The 500 Hidden Secrets of

VIENNA

INTRODUCTION

The aim of this book is to lead you to the best spots in Vienna, and to help you discover the city behind the idyllic, historic façade. On the one hand, Vienna is a dynamic, expanding capital in the centre of the current European Union, a city that has put itself on the map as a hot and happening place-to-be, with an exciting cultural scene, a trendy nightlife district and lots of innovative initiatives; on the other hand, its long historic heritage is tangible in its outstanding architecture, council housing, museums, theatres and festivals.

Vienna's city centre is manageable in terms of size, and pedestrian-friendly. You can easily explore it on foot or by bike; the city's beautiful parks and the banks of the Donau or the Donaukanal are perfect spots when you're in need of a rest. The metro system is one of the best in the world. And the city is safe: there are no no-go areas.

In this book, you'll learn some interesting facts about some of the city's timeless favourites; however most of the well-known tourist sights have been left out in favour of unexpected discoveries. The selection is subjective: these are the author's personal favourites that include some very secret gems, pop-up shops and daring art projects. She hopes that many of these addresses will be a pleasant surprise for visitors as well as locals, and that this book will lead to really experiencing that unique Vienna-feeling.

HOW TO
USE THIS BOOK?

———————

This guide lists 500 things you need to know about Vienna in 100 different categories. Most of these are places to visit, with practical information to help you find your way. Others are bits of information that help you get to know the city and its habitants. The aim of this guide is to inspire, not to cover the city from A to Z.

The places listed in the guide are given an address, including the neighbourhood, and a number. The neighbourhood and number allow you to find the locations on the maps at the beginning of the book: first look for the map of the corresponding neighbourhood, then look for the right number. The numbers of the maps do not correspond with the numbers of Viennas 23 districts that are spirally winding from the city centre (1) to Liesing (23). A word of caution: these maps are not detailed enough to allow you to find specific locations in the city. You can obtain an excellent map from any tourist office or in most hotels. Or the addresses can be located on a smartphone.

Please also bear in mind that cities change all the time. The chef who hits a high note one day may be uninspiring on the day you happen to visit. The hotel ecstatically reviewed in this book might suddenly go downhill under a new manager. Or the bar considered one of the '5 cocktail bars your should really try' might be empty on the night you visit. This is obviously a highly personal selection. You might not always agree with it. If you want to leave a comment, recommend a bar or reveal your favourite secret place, please visit the website *www.the500hiddensecrets.com* – you'll also find a lot of free tips and the latest news on the series there – or follow *@500hiddensecrets* on Instagram or Facebook and leave a comment.

THE AUTHOR

Tanja Paar wasn't born in Vienna but she has been living there for 25 years now, which is longer than she has lived in any other town. She started her career in writing and journalism working for diverse Austrian newspapers and magazines; she was a theatre critic for the Viennese weekly *Falter* and an editor for the daily *Der Standard*. She now works as a freelance writer and journalist. In February 2018 her first novel, *Die Unversehrten*, was published by Haymon Verlag. The book featured on the best-of-list of Austrian national broadcaster ORF for several months.

Tanja has lived in various corners of the city and now calls Leopoldstadt her home, the historic *Mazzesinsel* between the Donaukanal and the Donau. This cosy historic neighbourhood is only a 5-minute walk from the city centre and the green Prater park. Tanja loves to explore the city by bike. She knows every street and winding alley of Vienna and also enjoys hiking in the green hills and woods around the town.

The author wishes to thank all those who shared their insights and tips about Vienna. She also thanks the friends who visit her from all over the world and who she shows around the city, as well as her new neighbours from Syria and Iraq: thanks to them, she gets to look at her hometown with fresh eyes every day, always keeping in mind that her great-grandparents were immigrants in this town too.

Thanks to everyone at Luster and particularly to Dettie Luyten, for her kind guidance through the writing process of this book. Thanks to my partner Gerald for his patience and last but not least: thanks to my teenage son Leonard who provided me with the hottest tips about where to go out at night. He of course hopes his mom won't show up at these favourite venues of his, but you are most welcome. Enjoy!

VIENNA

overview

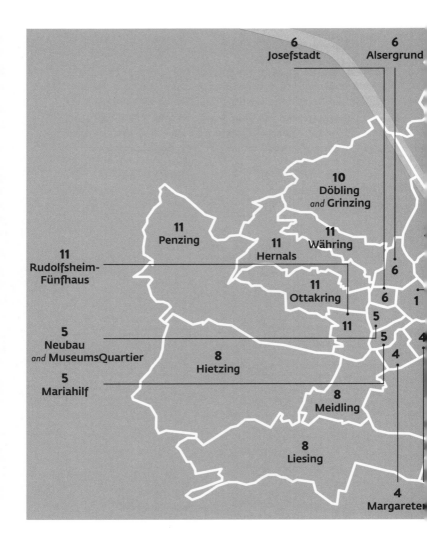

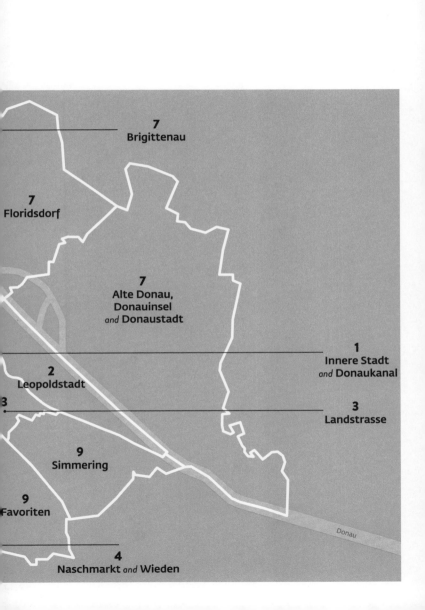

7
Brigittenau

7
Floridsdorf

7
Alte Donau,
Donauinsel
and Donaustadt

1
Innere Stadt
and Donaukanal

2
Leopoldstadt

3
Landstrasse

9
Simmering

9
Favoriten

4
Naschmarkt *and* Wieden

Donau

Map 1
INNERE STADT
and DONAUKANAL

EAT – **DRINK** – SHOP – FASHION & DESIGN – **BUILDINGS** – DISCOVER – **CULTURE** – CHILDREN – SLEEP – WEEKEND – RANDOM

Map 2
LEOPOLDSTADT

EAT – **DRINK** – SHOP – FASHION & DESIGN – **BUILDINGS** – DISCOVER – **CULTURE** – CHILDREN – SLEEP – WEEKEND – RANDOM

Map 3
LANDSTRASSE

Map 4
MARGARETEN,
NASCHMARKT and WIEDEN

Map 5
NEUBAU, MARIAHILF
and MUSEUMSQUARTIER

AT — **DRINK** — SHOP — FASHION & DESIGN — **BUILDINGS** — DISCOVER — **CULTURE** — CHILDREN — SLEEP — WEEKEND — **RANDOM**

Map 6
ALSERGRUND and
JOSEFSTADT

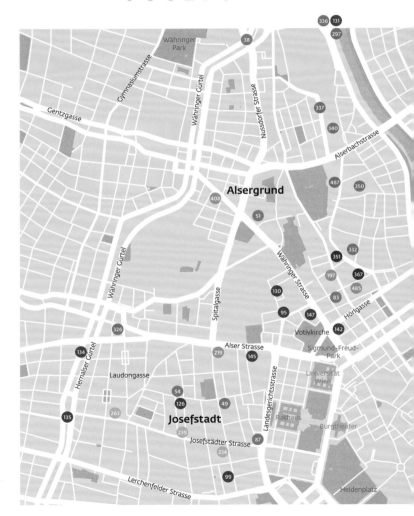

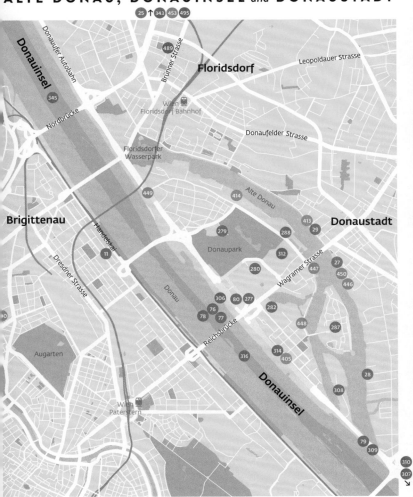

Map 8
HIETZING, LIESING *and* MEIDLING

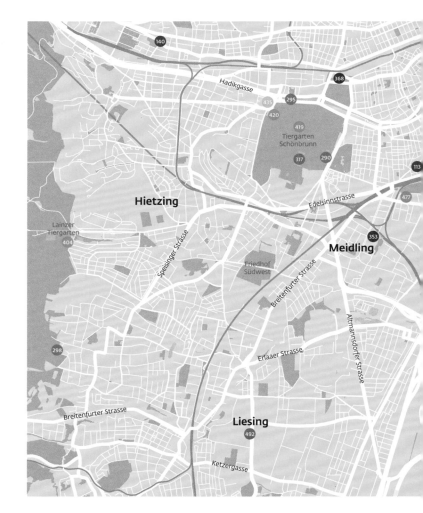

Hadikgasse

Tiergarten
Schönbrunn

Hietzing

Lainzer
Tiergarten

Edelsinnstrasse

Speisinger Strasse

Meidling

Friedhof
Südwest

Breitenfurter Strasse

Altmannsdorfer Strasse

Erlaaer Strasse

Breitenfurter Strasse

Liesing

Ketzergasse

Map 9
FAVORITEN and
SIMMERING

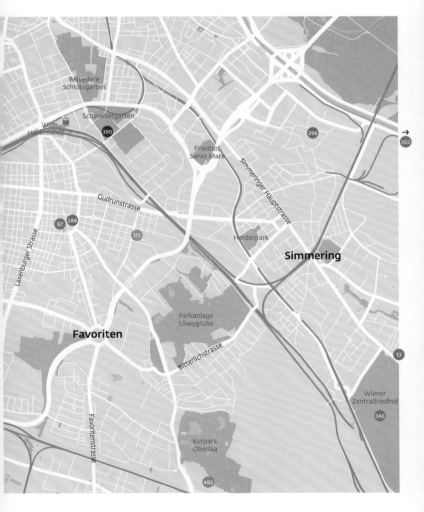

Balvedere Schlossgarten

Schweizergarten

Wien Hauptbahnhof

390

Friedhof Sankt Marx

296

→ 302

Simmeringer Hauptstrasse

Gudrunstrasse

Lavenburger Strasse

67 286

173

Herderpark

Simmering

Favoriten

Parkanlage Löwygrube

Bitterlichstrasse

13

Wiener Zentralfriedhof

346

Favoritenstrasse

Kurpark Oberlaa

482

Map 10
DÖBLING *and* GRINZING

Grinzing

Grinzinger
Friedhof

Grinzinger Strasse

Grinzinger Allee

Döbling

Sieveringer Strasse

Barawitzkagasse

Wertheimsteinpark

Donau

Heiligenstädter Strasse

Map 11
WEST
HERNALS, OTTAKRING, PENZING, RUDOLFSHEIM-FÜNFHAUS and WÄHRING

HABIBI & HAWARA

90 PLACES TO EAT OR BUY GOOD FOOD

5

SEAFOOD RESTAURANTS

you should definitely try

---

 1 **UMAR FISCH**
Naschmarkt 38-39
Naschmarkt ④
+43 (0)1 587 04 56
umarfisch.at

Erkan Umar originally opened a shop in Naschmarkt and nowadays he also has a small restaurant there. Still the best quality in town. Try to come on Monday, Wednesday or Friday when the fresh catch arrives. The counters with all the fresh seafood are definitely Insta-worthy.

2 **BRIUNI**
Blumauergasse 2
Leopoldstadt ②
+43 (0)1 968 32 57

As the Mediterranean is just 500 kilometres from Vienna, you can always score some fresh fish here. But nobody can match the price-quality ratio at Briuni (named after the beautiful Brijuni Islands). While the restaurant is Croatian, they also serve good pizza. Very down to earth, not *chichi* at all!

3 **VIKAS**
Wildpretmarkt 3
Innere Stadt ①
+43 (0)1 532 21 93
vikas.wien

Vikas is the place to go for fresh fish and seafood. Though it has been renovated, it has retained much of its traditional look and feel, with ropes, anchors and pictures of fishing boats on the wall. If this is your cup of tea, then look no further. A place you can safely take your mum! In the good sense.

4 SENHOR VINHO

Schwarzhorngasse 8
Margareten ④
+43 (0)1 545 84 00
senhorvinho.at

Senhor Vinho is a great Portuguese restaurant, where you can eat fresh fish or shrimp and the famous *bacalhau* (do try it but remember, it's quite salty). The tiny restaurant is like a little *Gesammtkunstwerk* with recommendations for Portuguese music, films, literature and travel. Do trust their tips because they know what they are talking about.

5 WULFISCH

Haidgasse 5
Leopoldstadt ②
+43 (0)1 946 18 75
wulfisch.at

Only 500 kilometres separate Vienna from the Adriatic but you'll need to drive almost 1000 kilometres to get to the North Sea. You can also feel this in the Viennese mentality. So when Wulfish launched a menu that featured crab rolls, pickled fish and herring salad everyone thought this was very exotic. Now everybody loves the stand-up-bar where you also can have a drink or two.

1 UMAR FISCH

5

VEGAN & VEGETARIAN

restaurants to visit

---

6 **HOLLEREI**
Hollergasse 9
Rudolfsheim-
Fünfhaus ⑪
+43 (0)1 892 33 56
hollerei.at

Holler is an abbreviation of *Holunder* which means elder tree. Elder brings good fortune which is why every farm used to have an elder tree. At Hollerei you can also get lucky thanks to the great seasonal vegetarian menu with Asian and Mediterranean influences. Book one of their cooking courses if you decide to stay on.

7 **CAFE HARVEST**
Karmeliterplatz 1
Leopoldstadt ②
+43 (0) 676 492 77 90
harvest-bistrot.at

Harvest is like a second living room for many locals. Become part of the family, it's so easy at this lovely place. Order a light snack or a coffee from Kaffee-rösterei Alt Wien with a homemade pastry. They also serve regional beers like a Schladminger BioZwickl or a local organic wine.

8 SWING KITCHEN

Schottenfeldgasse 3
Neubau ⑤
swingkitchen.com

Swing Kitchen is a vegan place. Since its opening in 2015, they have saved thousands of litres of water and tons of CO_2 by not using meat. They are very serious about their environmental efforts here. Charly Schillinger and his wife Irene were one of the first in Austria to prove that a vegan lifestyle can also offer plenty of culinary treats.

9 YAMM!

Universitätsring 10
Innere Stadt ①
+43 (0)1 532 05 44
yamm.at

Yamm! is conveniently located opposite the university which is why students love it so much. It's a big self-service restaurant, so you can easily drop in with a bigger group of 20 or 30 people. Very good quality, not super cheap but some great choices. As it's always quite crowded the food is very fresh.

10 GORILLA KITCHEN

Gusshausstrasse 19
Wieden ④
+43 (0)660 836 34 27
gorillakitchen.at

Burritos, bowls and sandwiches… A great place for street food behind the famous Karlskirche. They play hip-hop and punk music all day which is why you'll always see a youngish audience hanging out here. Not purists. You can order a vegan burrito or have meat. Here the rules are no extremism, no reservations. Come as you are!

5 places for famous
WIENER SCHNITZELS

11 **GASTHAUS KOPP**

Engerthstrasse 104
Brigittenau ⑦
+43 (0)1 330 43 92
gasthaus-kopp.at

There are many places in Vienna where you can eat a good Wiener schnitzel, but there is only one Gasthaus Kopp. This family restaurant opened in the sixties. Nowadays the Kopp and its humongous, delicious Wiener schnitzels are popular both with young people and the staff of the Lorenz Böhler hospital next door as the kitchen is open till 1 am.

12 **GASTHAUS AUTOMAT WELT**

Rueppgasse 19
Leopoldstadt ②
+43 (0)650 544 59 39
automat-welt.at

The name of this place was inspired by the Czech author Bohumil Hrabal's novel *Automat Svět*. You can read this book and many others in the restaurant. The chef works with organic ingredients only, sourcing his meat from local butchers. The menu is simple but it has one particularity. Here the Wiener schnitzels are made with *Schmalz* (lard). Hot and greasy!

13 CONCORDIA SCHLÖSSL

Simmeringer
Hauptstrasse 283
Simmering ⑨
+43 (0)1 769 88 88
concordia-schloessl.at

The best time to visit Concordia Schlössl is in November when Vienna is cold and foggy. The restaurant is located next door to the famous Wiener Zentralfriedhof, Austria's largest cemetery. Its morbid charm is extraordinary. They serve several variations on Wiener schnitzel here, including a *Fiakerschnitzel*, a *Käsekrainer* sausage wrapped in schnitzel.

14 WINKLERS ZUM POSTHORN

Posthorngasse 6
Landstrasse ③
+43 (0)664 431 21 23
*winklers-
zumposthorn.at*

The place to meet our president! While the Posthorn has been in business for several decades, Alexander Van der Bellen, Austria's newly-elected president, only moved in to his nearby flat very recently. At Winklers' they believe in treating Van der Bellen just like everyone else. The service is friendly and the *schnitzel* is nice.

✓ 15 GASTHAUS PÖSCHL

Weihburggasse 17
Innere Stadt ①
+43 (0)1 513 52 88
gasthauspöschl.com

Hanno Pöschl is a well-known Austrian actor. He loves to eat – you will understand when you see him – but what he loves best is to serve you an excellent *Wiener schnitzel* and other Austrian specialities like *Tafelspitz*, *Kümmelbraten* and *Rindsragout*. A lovely interior, very good service.

5 places to
EAT KOSHER

16 ALEF-ALEF
Seitenstettengasse 2
Innere Stadt ①
+43 (0)1 535 25 30
alefalef.at

As Vienna's Jewish population past and present tend to congregate in Vienna's second district Leopoldstadt on the so called *Mazzesinsel*, you'll also find most of the kosher restaurants here. The exception to this rule is Alef-Alef: enjoy a kosher Wiener schnitzel and *Apfelstrudel* in the centre of town. Very friendly staff.

20 MEA SHEARIM

17 NOVELLINO

Zirkusgasse 15
Leopoldstadt ②
+43 (0)1 212 81 69

Yes, there is such thing as kosher pizza in Vienna too. Find this discreet place on a corner in Leopoldstadt and feel as if you are in Willamsburg/New York. Many orthodox Jews eat here with their families but everyone else is also welcome.

18 BAHUR TOV

Taborstrasse 19
Leopoldstadt ②
+43 (0)676 847 761 200
bahur-tov.com

Bahur Tov is located near the middle of beautiful Taborstrasse where you can find many interesting shops. A great place for a break and some easy-going Middle Eastern food, with nothing grand or fancy about it. The food however tastes and looks amazing.

19 KOSHERLAND

Kleine Sperlgasse 6
Leopoldstadt ②
+43 (0)1 218 05 65

Kosherland is an oriental, kosher supermarket where you can also eat in. Here you can find everything you need to whip up a kosher meal. Some say it's even cheaper than in Israel. Try some of the tasty groceries. They also sell food and snacks from all over the world.

20 MEA SHEARIM

Schmelzgasse 3
Leopoldstadt ②
+43 (0)1 399 95 95
mea-shearim.at

If you like modern, Asian kosher cuisine, then this is definitely one for your list. Try an experimental sushi or maki roll, sample a kosher Aperol-Spritz or some tasty kosher wine. *Mea Shearim* is Hebrew and means one hundred gates as there are many different ways to enjoy a good meal.

The 5 best
HEURIGER

---

21 BUSCHENSCHANK IN RESIDENCE

Langackergasse 5-A
Grinzing ⑩
+43 (0)664 500 60 95
jutta-ambrositsch.at

Former graphic designer Jutta switched careers, becoming one of Austria's most interesting vintners, exporting her wine to New York among others. You can still sample her wine in her Buschenschank in Residence in Vienna, but only a few weekends of the year. Go for it!

22 HEURIGER HIRT

Eiserne Handgasse
Parzelle 165
Grinzing ⑩
+43 (0)1 318 96 41
heuriger-hirt.at

A place to go for the view, rather than the wine. A very traditional tavern, which has been in business for almost 90 years, in a very scenic location on top of the hill in Grinzing. Enjoy the walk up for some panoramic views of Vienna. You'll soon understand why they have so many regulars.

23 WIENINGER AM NUSSBERG

Eichelhofweg 125
Grinzing ⑩
+43 (0)664 854 70 22
wieninger-am-nussberg.at

This *Heuriger* also offers spectacular views of Vienna but is quite new (don't confuse it with the original Wieninger in Stammersdorf). As it burnt down two years ago – or was burnt down – they now serve drinks and delicious cold snacks from a container. Still one of the most beautiful places in town.

24 SCHANK ZUM REICHSAPFEL ✓

Karmeliterplatz 3
Leopoldstadt ②
+43 (0)1 212 25 79
zumreichsapfel.at

As *Heuriger* traditionally were only allowed to sell their own wine and products they usually are not situated in the city centre. This place, a *Stadtheuriger*, is different however as it's in the middle of town. The Reichsapfel looks like it's been here forever with its old wood panelling and quaint interior.

25 WEINHANDWERK

Senderstrasse 27
Floridsdorf ⑦
+43 (0)664 383 57 25
weinhandwerk.at

It's easy to spot why Weinhandwerk is different as the pink and yellow and green decoration scheme is very in your face. The building may be old but the spirit is entirely new. The young couple that took over the *Heuriger* have added an organic twist, serving good food made with foraged herbs and wine, which you can sample as you lay in hammocks. A great *Heuriger* to chill out!

25 WEINHANDWERK

5 *idyllic*
WATERFRONT TERRACES

---

26 MOTTO AM FLUSS
Franz Josefs Kai 2
Innere Stadt ①
+43 (0)1 252 55 10
mottoamfluss.at

Building modern architecture in Vienna's city centre can prove quite a challenge but BEHF Architects pulled it off, creating a landmark with this restaurant and cafe. The building looks like a futuristic ship at anchor along the *Donaukanal*. The restaurant offers some very good modern, international cuisine.

27 STRANDCAFÉ
Florian-Berndl-Gasse 20
Alte Donau ⑦
+43 (0)1 203 67 47
strandcafe-wien.at

The new Strandcafé opened in 2017 in a place that was famous for its grilled food for many years. Now the brand-new restaurant with its super large terrace and view of the Alte Donau still has Austria's biggest indoor grill, which is great in winter time when you can skate outside.

28 STRANDBEISL SELBST-VERSTÄNDLICH
An der Unteren Alten Donau 159
Alte Donau ⑦
+43 (0)1 204 39 69
strandbeisl.at

Built along a former branch of the Donau, the so-called Alte Donau, this restaurant has a beautiful waterfront terrace and serves typical Viennese food like *Ripperl* and Wiener schnitzel. Don't eat too much so you can still go for a swim in the clear water afterwards.

29 UFERTAVERNE

An der Oberen
Alten Donau 186
Alte Donau ⑦
+43 (0)1 204 39 53
ufertaverne.at

As the Donau doesn't flow anywhere near the city centre there are not that many waterfront terraces in Vienna. This is one of the most beautiful ones – with a long-standing tradition. Given its location behind a sailing school, generations of parents have sat and watched their children capsize here.

30 TEL AVIV BEACH

Obere Donau-
strasse 65
Leopoldstadt ①②
+43 (0)1 585 20 20
neni.at

Like so many temporary solutions in Vienna this one lasted. Haya Molcho and her team had the idea of bringing Tel Aviv's beach life to the Donaukanal for just one summer. But it proved so successful that they stayed on. The combo of Middle Eastern food, feet in the sand, DJs and a perfect spot to watch the sun set means this place is especially popular with the in-crowd.

26 MOTTO AM FLUSS

The 5 best
BURGERS
in Vienna

---

 31 **WEINSCHENKE**
Karmelitermarkt
Stand 10
Leopoldstadt ②
+43 (0)676 744 01 08
*weinschenke-
wien.com*

This place used to be called *Weinschenke* and the name stuck, which is funny as a *Weinschenke* is a place to drink cheap wine and get drunk as fast as possible. But that's their kind of humour! Not much on the menu but what you get is outstanding. And you get to sit in beautiful Karmelitermarkt.

32 **BURGER DE VILLE**
Lerchenfelder
Strasse 1-3
Neubau ⑤
25hours-hotels.com

Burger de Ville is a food truck in a park in front of the 25hours Hotel so it's not open in wintertime. In summertime, however, it's a popular spot for young people from nearby *Volkstheater* and *MuseumsQuartier*. Self-service, so just grab a jalapeño burger and find yourself a place to sit on a park bench.

33 **RINDERWAHN**
Weihburggasse 3
Innere Stadt ①
+43 (0)1 512 09 96
rinderwahn.at

Rinderwahn means mad cow disease. They have a great way with words here. Try their *Scharfe Resi* with chilli and pickles. A nice selection of craft beers, whisky and G&Ts. The *Schanigarten* outside was made using euro-pallets. Very laidback and easy-going.

34 HAFERPOINT

Gusshausstrasse 12
Wieden ④
+43 (0)1 920 44 54
haferpoint.com

Haferpoint originally was a place to feed the horses. *Hafer* means oats. Today this bright and airy place uses 100% Austrian meat for their burgers. Order their classic, American or spicy burger. The chicken burger is also yummy. No horse burger on the menu.

35 DIE BURGERMACHER

Burggasse 12
Neubau ⑤
+43 (0)699 115 895 99
dieburgermacher.at

Some say they serve the best burgers in town here. In any event, this is Vienna's fanciest burger joint. Very sleek, grey walls, no decoration, and some well-designed furniture. They have a nice selection of special beers (self-service too). The hipster factor is the only downside. Quite loud too.

35 DIE BURGERMACHER

5 original
WÜRSTELSTANDS

√36 **WÜRSTELSTAND AM HOHEN MARKT**
Hoher Markt 1
Innere Stadt ①
+43 (0)699 184 621 86

The *Käsekrainer* is the most famous of Vienna's street foods. The locals call it *Eitrige* and order it with a *Sechzehnerblech*, or a can of beer from the 16th district where the traditional Ottakringer brewery is located. Don't even try to pronounce this. Just point at the menu.

√37 **BITZINGER**
Albertinaplatz
Innere Stadt ①
+43 (0)660 815 24 13
bitzinger.at

As this place is located between the Opera House and Albertina, the world-famous gallery where you can see Albrecht Dürer's *Feldhase*, it's always very busy, even late at night. A fun place to meet singers, actors and barflies. Enjoy, but don't ask them for their autograph.

38 **WÜRSTEL LEO**
Döblinger Gürtel/
Nussdorfer Strasse
Alsergrund ⑥
+43 (0)664 659 60 85
wuerstelstandleo.at

As nearby Währinger Gürtel is lined with bars and concert venues, this *Würstelstand* is the spot for a late-night snack. This area used to be a red-light district – and maybe still is – but don't worry! Vienna doesn't really have any no-go areas so you can enjoy your sausages or hotdogs in peace.

39 ZUM SCHARFEN RENÉ

Schwarzenberg-
platz 15
Innere Stadt ①④
+43 (0)699 179 99888
zumscharfenrene.com

Scharf means hot, and René is hot and so are his *Debreziner, Burenhäutl* and *Pfefferoni*, which are all sausages with chilli pepper. You can choose your mustard though, either hot or sweet. Hang out here with people from the nearby theatre Kasino am Schwarzenbergplatz.

40 MARIAHILFER WURSTSTADL

Mariahilfer
Strasse 77
Mariahilf ⑤

Mariahilfer Strasse is one of Vienna's most important shopping streets, albeit not for the hidden secrets, but for the big chains. Head to nearby Neubaugasse for this typical Viennese snack. Bear in mind they don't serve any vegetarian options and there is no place to sit.

36 WÜRSTELSTAND AM HOHEN MARKT

5 excellent places for
FINE DINING

---

41 **CAFE ANSARI**

Praterstrasse 15
Leopoldstadt ②
+43 (0)1 276 51 02
cafeansari.at

Cafe Ansari is much more than a cafe. There is something distinctly French about it even though the owners, Nana and Nasser Ansari, originally hail from Georgia. They serve delicious Georgian and international dishes. The interior by the famous architect Gregor Eichinger is exquisite.

42 **RESTAURANT KONSTANTIN FILIPPOU**

Dominikaner-bastei 17
Innere Stadt ①
+43 (0)1 51 22 229
konstantin filippou.com

He saw, he came and he conquered. Konstantin Filippou opened his first own restaurant in 2013. In 2014, he earned his first Michelin star and in 2016, he was named chef of the year by Gault & Millau. Though his name sounds Greek he is Austrian, and his cuisine is international in the best and most purist sense. Excellent service.

43 ROOTS

Schönbrunner
Strasse 32
Margareten ④
+43 (0)660 242 40 65
bistroroots.at

Three young men, Miki Apostolo (Italian), Adam Benzce (Slovakian-Hungarian) and Marcus Walter (from the Austrian Salzkammergut) opened this place to celebrate their roots (they all worked for Filippou in the past). Here they serve a modern take on traditional recipes, working with the best local produce and according to the farm-to-table philosophy.

44 STEIRERECK √ IM STADTPARK

Am Heumarkt 2-A
Landstrasse ③
+43 (0)1 713 31 68
steirereck.at

Steirereck is Vienna's best and most famous restaurant. Familie Reitbauer and their team guarantee consistent quality. Try their *Meierei*, the small dependence in the middle of beautiful Stadtpark, where you can enjoy delicious food with a view of Wienfluss and Otto Wagner-Station.

45 ANNA SACHER

Philharmoniker-
strasse 4
Innere Stadt ①
+43 (0)1 514 568 40
sacher.com

The *Sacher* is the *Sacher* is the *Sacher*. Maybe that's the real secret of this place: that it always maintained an open-minded and international outlook ever since Anna Sacher – who was equally fond of cigars and her Old English Bulldogs – established its excellent reputation in the Fin de siècle. A first-rate place, with plenty of imperial grandeur.

5
ITALIAN PLACES
AMORE MIO

---

46 FABIOS
Tuchlauben 6
Innere Stadt ①
+43 (0)1 532 22 22
fabios.at

To see and be seen. This really could be the motto of this place where the rich and the beautiful meet. It's expensive but excellent. Lots of politicians love to lunch here. If Berlusconi was Austrian, he would love to eat lunch here too. Try the *Melanzane alla Parmigiana*.

47 PIZZA MARI
Leopoldsgasse 23-A
Leopoldstadt ②
+43 (0)676 687 49 94
pizzamari.at

Mari, the owner, wanted this place to be as Italian as possible – and boy, did she succeed. All the ingredients and recipes are Neapolitan, and she sticks to a rigid concept. They only serve pizza, *caffé* and sweets. And when they say *caffé* they mean *caffé*. No drinking cappuccinos after lunch here! The light is awful, but it only makes it feel even more like Napoli.

48 OSTERIA FRIULANA

Bartensteingasse 3
Innere Stadt ①
+43 (0)1 890 64 96
cantinafriulana.at

One of the best things to come out of Friuli, a region in northern Italy, is the *prosecco dalla spina*, which means sparkling wine on tap. And that is exactly how they serve it here at the Osteria. The food from this region can be quite heavy, compared with southern Italy. So order a savoury mix of *sarde in saór* and *prosciutto San Daniele*.

49 OLIVA VERDE

Florianigasse 15
Josefstadt ⑥
+43 (0)676 681 81 72
olivaverde.at

There are plenty of Italian restaurants in Vienna but only a few have stood the test of time and Oliva verde is one of them. The quality of the food they serve has always been consistent and this tiny place behind city hall has always stuck to its guns, with affordably-priced good food.

50 WETTER

Payergasse 13/
Yppenplatz
Ottakring ⑪
+43 (0)1 406 07 75
wettercucina.at

Wetter is not your typical Italian restaurant. Raetus Wetter serves *cucina povera*, including tripe, while his wife Lea Redolf is a wine expert. Do follow her advice. The atmosphere is quite laidback. A view of beautiful Yppenplatz, no tablecloths, no cloth napkins.

The 5 most classic
ASIAN RESTAURANTS

51 **KIM**

**Währinger
Strasse 46
Alsergrund** ⑥
+43 (0)664 425 88 66
sohyikim.com

When Kim arrived in Vienna from Korea, she didn't have a penny to her name. So she began to cook in a very tiny place near Volksoper and soon her delicious meals became famous. With only five small tables and a multi-course dinner consisting of raw fish only (not sushi!) she became a star. Do visit and get to know her personally.

52 **CHINA BAR**

**Burggasse 76
Neubau** ⑤
chinabar.at

Simon Xie Hong is a Chinese doctor. As he was not allowed to practise in his profession in Austria, he decided to work as a chef in a small mountainside village instead. As he found it difficult to source the ingredients he needed, he developed his own experimental fusion cuisine, which is still very unique today. He has opened two more restaurants since but China Bar, the first one, is still our favourite.

53 MOCHI

Praterstrasse 15
Leopoldstadt ②
+43 (0)1 925 13 80
mochi.at

Mochi brought a bit of Berlin style to Vienna. A very casual, down-to-earth place, where beer is served in the bottle, and a first come, first serve policy at lunch. Indoor it can be a bit pokey, but the extraordinary Japanese food soon makes you forget any reservations you have. Sit under the wonderful old trees outside.

54 SAKAI

Florianigasse 36
Josefstadt ⑥
+43 (0)1 729 65 41
sakai.co.at

The owner Hiroshi Sakai spent many years working as the chef of the famous Unkai in Vienna's Grandhotel before he decided to strike out on his own. Now we are lucky to have this real *Kappo* (Japanese restaurant), with six pages of appetisers no less. Just tell the chef how many of you there are and let him put together a menu for you. It's worth it.

55 SEOUL

Praterstrasse 26
Leopoldstadt ②
+43 (0)1 218 65 28

As you might have guessed from its name, Seoul is a Korean restaurant. While it does not look fancy from the outside, it would be a mistake to walk by and miss it. This tiny restaurant is always crowded (Korean ex-pats and locals). Don't worry, it's not you, the owner is always this unfriendly. But the food! The food!

The 5 best places for
FOODIES

---

56 HABIBI & HAWARA ✓

Wipplinger-
strasse 29
Innere Stadt ①
+43 (0)1 535 06 75
habibi.at

Habibi means friend in Arabic – and
Hawara means exactly the same in
Viennese dialect. In this case the name
reveals more about the restaurant's
intentions. Here Orient meets Vienna
and refugees cook for the locals. It looks
like *1001 Nights* and has a certain *Schmäh*
– a certain kind of humour – to it. The
owner Katha Schinkinger guarantees that
the service is excellent.

57 RAMASURI

Praterstrasse 19
Leopoldstadt ②
+43 (0)676 466 80 60
ramasuri.at

Ramasuri means chaos, but the kind of
chaos that's fun. As if a nice surprise or
something you didn't expect falls into
your lap. This colourful restaurant is
a bit like this. Young people serve various
seasonal dishes (five different breakfasts
till late, try the Avocadolala). Even more
beautiful when you sit outside in the
tiny square.

58 PROSI INDIAN RESTAURANT

Kandlgasse 44
Neubau ⑤
+43 (0)1 522 44 44
prosiindian
restaurant.at

You can't visit Vienna without stopping at Prosi. It was and is still the premium place to buy food from all over the world: beans from Mexico, plantain from Africa, spices from India. The shop was so successful that they opened another one for beauty products. Now they also have a restaurant. Enjoy a taste of the world.

59 BABETTE'S SPICE AND BOOKS FOR COOKS

Am Hof 13
Innere Stadt ①
+43 (0)1 533 66 85
babettes.at

Babette's is a stroke of luck. If you love cookbooks, spices and good food, then this place is your personal heaven. They have a good selection of books, plenty of fresh spices, but only three tables. So you need to get very lucky to nab one. If not, buy some books and come again.

60 ZUM FINSTEREN STERN

Schulhof 8
Innere Stadt ①
+43 (0)1 535 21 00
zumfinsterenstern.at

The owner Ella De Silva is a mysterious woman. She always succeeds in creating something special. The name of her restaurant refers to her first business in Vienna, a winery in Sterngasse where she used to cook on a single electric hot plate. Now she has a kitchen – and a beautiful courtyard to sit in in summer.

5 breaths of fresh air:
OUTDOOR DINING

---

61 VILLA AURORA
Wilhelminen-
strasse 237
Ottakring ⑪
+43 (0)1 489 33 33

Villa Aurora is like an elegant, old lady. You love and admire her even though she can be a bit of a nuisance. The restaurant is not perfect, but the Villa is so beautiful, the old furniture so stylish and the view is simply to die for. In summer you can sit in the garden and it feels like you have travelled back in time.

62 VOLKSGARTEN ✓ PAVILLON
Volksgarten
Innere Stadt ①
+43 (0)1 532 09 07
volksgarten-pavillon.at

The Volksgarten Pavillon dates from the sixties – and was retro before retro was trendy. How lucky we are that it was never renovated but allowed to retain its *chic*. Sit at metal tables with original sixties lamps in a beautiful garden in the middle of town. Even the petanque court is original.

63 GLACIS BEISL

Breite Gasse 4
Neubau ⑤
+43 (0)1 526 56 60
glacisbeisl.at

Some people have likened Glacis Beisl in MuseumsQuartier to a UFO. But in this case the UFO is the old object in between all the modern buildings like mumok, Kunsthalle and Leopold Museum. It was here first however and is part of the old *Glacis*, the former medieval parade ground outside the city walls. Sit under the very old trees to get a sense of history.

64 SCHWEIZERHAUS

Karl-Kolarik-Weg
Prater 116
Leopoldstadt ②
+43 (0)1 728 01 52
schweizerhaus.at

The Schweizerhaus is a cult place. Vienna's mayor traditionally comes here on May 1st after the parade for a pork knuckle. The place is only open in summertime (mid-March till October) as it is a large beer garden. It's such a big place that you can easily get lost – if you are drunk that is. Then again, this is definitely feasible given their excellent Budweiser Budvar.

65 RESTAURANT TEMPEL

Praterstrasse 56
Leopoldstadt ②
+43 (0)1 214 01 79
restaurant-tempel.at

There is no temple here. But the original restaurant was located in Tempelgasse just a few streets over in Jewish Leopoldstadt. The chef cooks his own experimental take on Austrian classics using only the best ingredients. The courtyard is beautiful – but try to keep your voice down for the neighbours.

5 tasty
ICE CREAMS

---

66 EIS GREISSLER √
Rotenturm-
strasse 13
Innere Stadt ①
eis-greissler.at

There is always a queue here. *Eis Greissler* has different shops in Austria and their Vienna branch is very small. But the wait is so worth it! All the milk comes from their own organic farm in Krumbach. The ice cream is simply delicious. Try their new flavours, beetroot and juniper, which blend very nicely with gin.

67 TICHY
Reumannplatz 13
Favoriten ⑨
+43 (0)1 604 44 46
gastroweb.at/tichy-eis

In 1952, Kurt and Marianne Tichy opened their first shop in Vienna. Now, many years later, they have moved to Reumannplatz, giving you two reasons to visit it: the beautiful art deco Amalienbad that was built in 1923 and the original *Tichy Eis-Marillenknödel* (ice-apricot-dumplings).

✓ 68 EISSALON TUCHLAUBEN

Tuchlauben 15
Innere Stadt ①
+43 (0)1 533 25 53
eissalon-
tuchlauben.at

Eissalon Tuchlauben is a classic. Lots of children from the nearby schools are regulars. This has been the temple of ice cream since 1962, serving classic flavours like *Amarena* and *Stracciatella*, as well as bolder and experimental flavours like nougat and cornel cherry.

69 GEFRORENES

Währinger
Strasse 152
Währing ⑪
+43 (0)699 192 562 05
gefrorenes.at

Gefrorenes means frozen and their philosophy is to serve good ice cream like in the old days. Here you can take your pick from 20 different types of ice cream and special *éclairs* like 'Vanilla Tonka-Bohnen Éclair', salted caramel *éclair* and hazelnut *éclair*. They also have elegant retro boxes so you can take some home with you.

70 GELATERIA LA ROMANA

Stiftgasse 15-17
Neubau ⑤
+43 (0)1 523 23 00
gelateriaromana.com

Gelateria La Romana is a real Italian gelateria. Their home town is Rimini, the heart of the Italian dream of the fifties. But Ivano and Massimiliano Zucchi have remained faithful to tradition, serving all the traditional flavours. They only use recycled packaging. *Buonissimo* and environmentally-friendly, too.

5 times only in Vienna:
SCHANIGÄRTEN

---

71 ULRICH
St. Ulrichsplatz 1
Neubau ⑤
+43 (0)1 961 27 82
ulrichwien.at

Some Viennese history to understand Viennas *Schanigärten*: *Schani* is a nickname for Johann, and a popular name among waiters. They had to carry the tables and chairs in and out every day to and from the garden. Nowadays most *Schanigartens* are open from March 1st until November 15th. Ulrich is of the most beautiful ones.

72 CHINA BAR ✓
AN DER WIEN
Hamburger-
strasse 2
Naschmarkt ④
+43 (0)1 971 32 88
chinabaranderwien.at

As Naschmarkt is one of Vienna's most traditional farmer's markets you should come here on a Saturday, when there is a flea market in the area too. From this *Schanigarten*, you can enjoy a fantastic view of the street and the beautiful Jugendstil buildings at the other end of the street.

73 KLEE AM
HANSLTEICH
Amundsen-
strasse 10
Hernals ⑪
+43 (0)1 480 51 50
klee.wien

Klee is a bit like a trip to the countryside without leaving the city: you sit on the banks of the Hanselteich, a small lake, with the fresh air of the nearby Wiener-wald. On cold winter days, the skaters on the frozen lake make it look even more like a Brueghel painting.

74 PALMENHAUS

Burggarten 1
Innere Stadt ①
+43 (0)1 533 10 33
palmenhaus.at

Palmenhaus is extraordinary. This greenhouse for the emperor's gardens was built in 1901 in the middle of the city right behind Hofburg. Today it's home to a butterfly garden and a spectacular brasserie where you can sit under the Jugendstil steel structure or in front of the building in lovely Burggarten.

75 KLEINES CAFÉ

Franziskanerplatz 3
Innere Stadt ①

Kleines Café is tiny. Here you won't find any trees or flowers, but the cafe gives out onto a beautiful square where the Renaissance Franziskanerkirche rises up like a flower above the square. The view rather than the food makes this place special. No reservations, no complaints, just enjoy.

74 PALMENHAUS

The 5 best places
ON DONAUINSEL

76 **TAVERNE SOKRATES**
AT: SUNKEN CITY
**Wiener Haupt-
strasse 60-B
Donauinsel** ⑦
+43 (0)1 587 41 11
restaurant-sokrates.at

Taverne Sokrates is a slice of Greece in Vienna. From the terrace you can see the water of the Donau sparkle in the distance and with a bit of imagination you can even think that you are at the seaside. The picture becomes even more perfect when the *suflaki*, squid and other Greek specialities arrive on your plate. A little like *My Big Fat Greek Wedding*!

77 **SANSIBAR**
AT: SUNKEN CITY
Donauinsel ⑦
+43 (0)660 777 30 11
sansibar.co.at

Sansibar is like the African Island: colourful, loud and hot. It is situated near Taverne Sokrates so you can have dinner here and then go for a drink. The music is a mix of Latin, hip-hop and reggaeton. A young crowd, globetrotters and *Hawaras* from Vienna have a good time in this beach club.

78 **PORTO POLLO**
**Donauinsel 19
Donauinsel** ⑦

Porto Pollo is definitely not mainstream. It is located near the Donau where there is also a small harbour for motorboats, a *porto*. Drinks only. If you want barbecue you have to book beforehand. Reservations can only be made in person.

79 WAKE_UP

Am Wehr 1
Donauinsel ⑦
+43 (0)1 202 51 23
wakeup.at

Wake_up is the restaurant and bar near Vienna's one and only wakeboard lift. Enjoy the waterfront views and the acrobatics of the wakeboarders on Neue Donau, a branch of the Donau. A great place for a light snack or dinner with your feet in the sand. Breakfast till 1 pm, P&R and metro (U2) nearby.

80 57 RESTAURANT LOUNGE

DC Tower
Donaustadt ⑦
57melia.com

This restaurant and lounge is situated on the 57th floor of Austria's tallest building. Definitely the place with the most spectacular view of the Donauinsel and the city of Vienna. The bar is located on top of the restaurant. Here they serve 30 different cocktails, focussing on regional products like Wien Gin.

78 PORTO POLLO

5 great places to have
BRUNCH

---

81 **HEALTH KITCHEN**
   Zollergasse 14
   Neubau ⑤
   +43 (0)664 345 62 97
   myhealthkitchen.com

Can fast food be healthy? Yes! As Health Kitchen proves, with locally-sourced, organic, low-carb food, that is always fresh and tasty. Reservations required for groups of 7 or more people as the place is tiny. A brunch buffet is served on Sundays and holidays.

82 **NENI**
   Naschmarkt 510
   Naschmarkt ④
   +43 (0)1 585 20 20
   neni.at

Have an oriental brunch at Nenis in the lovely but crowded Naschmarkt. On Saturdays it can get very busy here. Enjoy being part of the young, international crowd. What's nice is, you can even stay for lunch and dinner.

83 FLORENTIN ✓

Berggasse 8
Alsergrund ⑥
+43 (0)676 735 56 25
florentin1090.com

Berggasse is an historic place. Sigmund Freud lived and worked here before he fled the Nazis. And Café Berg, one of Vienna's first gay restaurants, opened its doors here. Now this place is called Florentin, where you can enjoy tasty, Mediterranean, mostly organic food. Start your day here with a brunch before visiting the Freud Museum.

84 LE BOL ✓

Neuer Markt 15
Innere Stadt ①
+43 (0)699 103 018 99
lebol.at

Le Bol is a slice of France in Vienna. It was the first place to sell proper French croissants in the city. Try their *Petit dejeuner du Baou* with a *Croque Monsieur* and an onion soup. Reservations must be made in person.

85 OBEN

Urban-Loritz-Platz 2-A
Neubau ⑤
+43 (0)1 522 72 68
oben.at

Many people come here for the stellar view. The OBEN is located on the top floor of Vienna's public library which was designed by the architect Ernst Mayr. The light glass-membrane structure with a monumental platform reminds us of Casa Malaparte. If you love food, books and modern architecture, this place ticks all the boxes.

85 OBEN

5

COFFEE HOUSES

to do some people watching

---

 86 **CAFE BRÄUNERHOF**
Stallburggasse 2
Innere Stadt ①
+43 (0)1 512 38 93

Rule number one in a typical Viennese *Kaffeehaus*: the waiters are rude! And the Bräunerhof is no exception to the rule. So don't take it too personally. The famous Austrian writer Thomas Bernhard loved to come here. Read some of his books and you will better understand the special mentality in this place.

87 **CAFÉ EILES**
Josefstädter
Strasse 2
Josefstadt ⑥
+43 (0)1 405 34 10
cafe-eiles.at

The Eiles is another traditional *Kaffeehaus*. Many writers and actors come here to read, write, discuss, have lunch, start an affair or end one. They recently started hiring refugees as waiters – who are not rude at all. This is the only thing that is not typically Viennese about this place. Enjoy!

88 CAFÉ PRÜCKEL √

Stubenring 24
Innere Stadt
+43 (0)1 512 611 512
prueckel.at

Café Prückel is a wonderful fifties-style place, the interior is original and is a listed monument. Don't be rude to the waiters. Many writers and journalists come here for interviews. Some of them are famous. Just ignore them.

89 CAFE KORB √

Brandstätte 9
Innere Stadt ①
+43 (0)1 533 72 15
cafekorb.at

Those writers, journalists and actors who don't frequent Bräunerhof or Prückel can be found at Cafe Korb. The only difference is that this is more of an arty-farty place. The owner Susanne Widl is an artist and is friends with many other artists like Peter Weibel, Günter Brus and Elfriede Gerstl who like this place. Still rocking!

90 CAFE ENGLÄNDER √

Postgasse 2
Innere Stadt ①
+43 (0)1 966 86 65
cafe-englaender.com

Everyone is treated equally at the Engländer (which means the Englishman), regardless of who they are. The waiters are friendly if you are. Popular with many writers, actors and journalists. Patti Smith, Yoko Ono and John Malkovich have been spotted here. A place where you can eat, laugh and talk until late.

SUPERSENSE

65 PLACES TO GO OUT AND HAVE A DRINK

5 places to go
TANGO DANCING

---

91 KUNSTTANKSTELLE OTTAKRING
Grundstein-
gasse 45-47
Ottakring ⑥
*kunsttankstelle
ottakring.at*

All the milongas in Vienna are a great place to go dancing or to watch other people dance while enjoying a drink. Kunsttankstelle used to be a fuel station, today it's a 'culture station'. A weird sixties style, the artsy people from nearby Brunnenmarkt like to drop in too.

92 BARADA
Robert Hamerling-
Gasse 1
Rudolfsheim-
Fünfhaus ⑥
tango-vienna.at

Barada is a beautiful historic hall with beautiful ceiling ornaments, which is tucked away in an old courtyard near Westbahnhof. Here you can learn all about oriental dance, barefoot dance and every second Friday Satho-Sabine and Thomas host tango lessons. Enjoy the traditional milonga and the homemade sweets.

93 ROTE BAR IM VOLKSTHEATER

Neustiftgasse 1
Neubau ⑤
+43 (0)1 522 37 80
volkstheater.at

Volkstheater is one of Vienna's most important historic theatres. It has a red and a white bar, called the Rote Bar and Weisser Salon. You should check out both. The Rote Bar often hosts concerts and different kind of dance parties. The Crossover-Milonga is one of the most spectacular events.

94 GALERIA IDEAL

Geibelgasse 14
Rudolfsheim-
Fünfhaus ⑪
galeria-ideal.at

Step inside Galeria Ideal and you may be forgiven for thinking you've landed in Buenos Aires. This place is located in a former industrial hall and has retained its industrial chic style. The comfortable sofas are a great place to sit and chat over a glass of excellent Argentinean wine.

95 ALBERT SCHWEITZER HAUS

Schwarzspanier-
strasse 13
Alsergrund ⑥
+43 (0)1 408 34 09
tangobar.at

Albert Schweitzer Haus is named after the famous doctor and theologian. Today it's a student dorm with a nice public restaurant in it. You sit around an atrium, watch people dancing (tango every Thursday) or have a drink or two at the bar.

5 places under the
RAINBOW FLAG

───────

√ 96 **CAFÉ SAVOY**
Linke Wienzeile 36
Naschmarkt ④
+43 (0)1 581 15 57
savoy.at

Café Savoy is a traditional *Kaffeehaus* with magnificent gilt mirrors so it is definitely worth visiting, regardless of your sexual orientation. Everybody is welcome here. It's near Naschmarkt and on sunny days you can sit outside and observe the colourful streetlife.

√ 97 **ROSA LILA VILLA**
Linke Wienzeile 102
Naschmarkt ④
dievilla.at

Like the *Venus of Willendorf*, the Café Willendorf in the Villa is sensuous – and it is also a historic place. It was one of the first places in Vienna to fly the rainbow flag. You would not believe it, but at one time Vienna was a drab, narrow-minded, ugly place. The Villa helped change this.

98 **WHY NOT**
Tiefer Graben 22
Innere Stadt ①
why-not.at

The Why Not is a gay late-night club where you can have fun dancing and have a drink. It's in the middle of town, tucked away in Tiefer Graben, next to the famous Hotel Orient where you can have a discreet one-night stand. Nobody in Vienna ever was here but it's always booked up.

99 FRAUEN CAFÉ √

Lange Gasse 11
Josefstadt ⑥
frauencafe.com

The F*C is a queer-feminist space. It's organised in a basic-democratic way. It opened in 1977, making it one of the oldest establishments of its kind in Austria. Generations of women have met here to discuss and organise themselves. Nowadays it is a LGBT space where you can meet other people if you are new to Vienna.

100 FETT & ZUCKER √

Hollandstrasse 16
Leopoldstadt ②
+43 (0)699 116 600 92
fettundzucker.at

Fett & Zucker means fat & sugar – and boy, do they deliver. This place is a bakery and a cafe. But it's much more than that. It's a queer and lesbian-friendly hangout but that doesn't really matter as long as you are wild and free and love sweets and don't give a shXX about body standards in general. Enjoy!

96 CAFÉ SAVOY

5

HIPSTER BARS

---

101 WIRR

Burggasse 70
Neubau ⑤
wirr.at

Wirr means confused. But it isn't. It is a bar (good cocktails), a restaurant and a club (downstairs). Hipsters love it but the young urban crowd doesn't make you feel too bad if you're not a trendy urbanite. They serve breakfast until 4 pm.

102 AN DO

Yppenplatz 11-15
Ottakring ⑪
+43 (0)1 308 75 75
cafeando.at

An Do in Yppenplatz is another hipster hangout. Actually, the whole of Yppenplatz is uber-trendy but An Do is like the eye of the hurricane. Everything moves and changes except for An Do, which always remains the same. Simple but yummy Levantine food, relaxed service. Don't be in a hurry, be cool.

103 SUPERSENSE

Praterstrasse 70
Leopoldstadt ②
+43 (0)1 969 08 32
supersense.com

Supersense is a bar, a cafe and a concept store. Here you can buy fancy instant print cameras, LPs or record your own LP in the studio in the shop. The bar and cafe have a nice menu, they often host special events with famous cooks or simple Thai street food. Let them surprise you.

104 BALTHASAR

Praterstrasse 38
Leopoldstadt ②
+43 (0)664 381 68 55
balthasar.at

The concept is deliciously simple: the best coffee (baristas love it), sparkling wine and a few snacks. That's all. A fashionable, gold blue and white interior. Excellent Wi-Fi. There aren't always enough seats, self-service. Hipsters from the nearby hubs and agencies start their day here. Open till 7 pm.

105 VOLLPENSION

Schleifmühlgasse 16
Naschmarkt ④
vollpension.wien

Where did you get the best biscuits as a child? At your nan's of course. Vollpension decided to remind everyone of this rule. *Pension* means retirement in German and *Vollpension* is a play on words. Grandma is the chef at this transgenerational cafe where you can sample some of the best sweets in town.

103 SUPERSENSE

The 5 most laidback
BEACH BARS

---

106 STRANDBAR HERRMANN

Herrmannpark
Donaukanal ①
+43 (0)720 229 996
strandbarherrmann.at

Located opposite Urania Sternwarte this beach cafe is the perfect place for sunset drinks. *Herrmann* gets the most sun, so plan to spend the evening here. Enjoy a snack or a cocktail with your feet in the sand. They have a big screen for football matches.

107 HAFENKNEIPE

Untere Donau-strasse 47
Donaukanal ①
+43 (0)699 113 535 68

Hafenkneipe is a little rough around the edges. Essentially this is just a container with some deckchairs around it – but it is one of the most relaxed places along the Donaukanal. You can order drinks, homemade pizza if the mobile pizza oven is around and sometimes *Steckerlfisch*, a local speciality (fish grilled on a stick). The best sunset in town.

108 ADRIA

Obere Donau-strasse 97-99
Donaukanal ①
adriawien.at

Adria means Adriatic Sea. They were the first to introduce the Italian lifestyle along the Donaukanal. Enjoy the large terrace, the deck chairs, the Thai snacks or pasta. They are open also in winter as they have a large winter garden. Pioneers of the brave-hearted kind. Simply the best.

109 BADESCHIFF

Donaukanal
Donaukanal ①
+43 (0)660 312 47 03
badeschiff.at

Badeschiff is unique in Vienna. As the laws are very strict here, there are no houseboats on the canals and rivers like in Amsterdam. So Badeschiff is the only boat on the Donaukanal – and it has a pool too. You can swim here, have a snack on the deck, or lunch or dinner on the lounge deck. Also open in winter.

110 SUMMERSTAGE

Rossauer Lände
Donaukanal ①
+43 (0)1 319 66 44
summerstage.at

The Summerstage is a Viennese classic. Oswald Schellmann started out with a small outdoor venue, but now the pavilion here is open all year long, with different cafes and restaurants, art and sports events, live gigs, wine tasting and much more. It is a world unto its own – and it is a beautiful world.

108 ADRIA

5 great
BEER BARS

---

111 1516 BREWING-COMPANY

Schwarzenberg-
strasse 2
Innere Stadt ①
+43 (0)1 961 15 16
1516brewing
company.com

1516 Brewing Company brews ales and beers from malted barley but also uses malted and unmalted wheat, rice or rye, when necessary. Which is quite special. But this place is special too. You can order an excellent burger here, made with beef from the Austrian Alps. Wash it down with a beer. *Prost!*

112 MEL'S CRAFT BEERS & DINER

Wipplingerstrasse 9
Innere Stadt ①
paddysco.at

Here they already had an extensive range of Austrian and international craft beers before this became a hype – as well as some great food. The revolution in the beer industry is the merit of the many microbreweries around the world. Here you can celebrate their victory over bland lager beers.

113 BEER STORE VIENNA

Wilhelmstrasse 23
Meidling ⑧
+43 (0)1 974 46 27
beerstorevienna.at

There is something going on in Favoriten: Beer Store is the only place in Vienna where you can find the equipment and expertise to start brewing your own home brews. They also have many speciality beers and a tap room where you can try all 170 beers for just one euro.

114 REINWEIN

Reindorfgasse 10
Rudolfsheim-
Fünfhaus ⑪
+43 (0)650 211 81 93
reinwein.wien

Their name refers to wine and in fact this place is the perfect combination of a *Vinothek* and a craft beer bar. You can find a selection of great Austrian wines and 66 different national and international craft beers here. Lovely interior with plenty of books.

115 MUTTERMILCH VIENNA BREWERY

Gumpendorfer
Strasse 35
Mariahilf ⑤
muttermilchbrewery.at

They are the hippest: Muttermilch c/o Beer Lovers is the hottest bar in town – if you like beer that is. Follow a brewing workshop with expert Marina Ebner and beer sommelier Markus Betz and get a diploma. Did you know *Muttermilch* means breast milk?

5 exciting
WINE BARS

116 **UNGER UND KLEIN**
Gölsdorfgasse 2
Innere Stadt ①
+43 (0)1 532 13 23
ungerundklein.at

A golden oldie. The Unger und Klein and its famous, timeless architecture (Eichinger oder Knechtl) has been in business for more than 20 years. It is still one of the best wine bars in town. The owner Michi Klein and Helmuth Unger like to chat with their regulars, so make you become one of them.

117 **PUB KLEMO WEINBAR**
Margaretenstrasse 61
Margareten ④
+43 (0)699 110 913 32
pubklemo.at

There is wine of course. But they serve spirits too. Have a cold snack or enjoy the homemade pasta. Order a glass of wine or buy the whole bottle: do you need an easy wine or something rarer? They will gladly advise you. They also have a Pub Klemo Shop and a branch along the Donaukanal in summer.

118 **WEIN & CO BAR**
Linke Wienzeile 4
Naschmarkt ④
+43 (0)5 0706 3102
weinco.at

Wein & Co is a very well-stocked shop as well as a bar. There are a few in town, but the one at the corner of Naschmarkt, with its famous golden *Sezession* dome, is the best. People love to have an after-work drink here. Stay a little longer.

119 ZUM SCHWARZEN ✓ KAMEEL

Bognergasse 5
Innere Stadt ①
+43 (0)1 533 81 25
kameel.at

No, this is not a spelling error. *Kameel* is written with two e's. The black camel has graced the logo of this place since 1618. It is so beautiful. The *azulejos*, or ceramic tiles, will make you feel as if you have stepped into a set from *1001 Nights* – but the wine and the famous *Brötchen* are typically Viennese. Where Bourgeoisie meets Pop.

120 MEINLS WEINBAR ✓

Graben 19
Innere Stadt ①
+43 (0)1 532 33 34
meinlamgraben.at

Like Kameel, Meinl is a classic in Vienna. Meinl am Graben still is the most famous gourmet food store with a history that goes back to imperial times. The building itself is a listed monument, so do have a good look at it. Try a glass of delicious Austrian wine.

119 ZUM SCHWARZEN KAMEEL

5

COCKTAIL BARS

you should really try

---

121 FIRST FLOOR
Seitenstettengasse 5
Innere Stadt ①
+43 (0)1 532 11 65
firstfloorbar.at

The most astonishing feature of the beautiful interior of this bar is the huge aquarium that dominates the room. It lines the wall behind the bar like a living picture. It also makes the atmosphere here quite special, in combination with the warm brown wood panelling. Mind your step when you walk down again.

121 FIRST FLOOR

122 LOOSBAR

Kärntner Durch-
gang 10
Innere Stadt ①
+43 (0)1 512 32 83
loosbar.at

Loosbar or Loos American Bar was
actually designed by the famous architect
Adolf Loos in 1908 – and it still is a gem.
The room only measures 4,40 × 6,00 ×
4,10 metres, but it's always crowded.
Its interior is a modern classic. Going
to the loo downstairs is even more
dangerous than on the first floor. Mind
the steep chairs!

123 INTERMEZZO BAR

Johannesgasse 28
Innere Stadt ①
+43 (0)1 711 22 0
vienna.
intercontinental.com

The USP of Intermezzo Bar is the
enormous chandelier that hangs over the
bar. It's simply unique. The Interconti
Vienna was built in the sixties, which
also explains its design style. The hotel
is thinking of revamping so see the bar
while it is still there.

124 SILVERBAR

Wiedner Haupt-
strasse 12
Wieden ④
+43 (0)1 589 181 33
dastriest.at

The Silverbar is located in hotel Triest:
a nice, urban design hotel. You don't
have to stay here to enjoy their excellent,
well-stocked bar. Bar manager Keita from
Senegal guarantees only the very highest
quality. Celebrities also like to hang out
here. Cash only.

125 ROBERTO AMERICAN BAR

Bauernmarkt 11-13
Innere Stadt ①
+43 (0)1 535 06 47
robertosbar.com

Even the homepage of this place is slick.
A black sign with a statement reading
'Come and see for yourself'. Word of
mouth does the trick. And it works.
Everybody in town is talking about
Roberto's Bar and everybody is happy that
there is another place for *connoisseurs*.

5 places if you're partying
ON A BUDGET

126 TUNNEL

Florianigasse 39
Josefstadt ⑥
+43 (0)1 990 44 00
tunnel-vienna-live.at

The Tunnel is a world unto itself. Many generations of students have had drinks, have eaten or partied here but somehow it always manages to offer something new. It manages to transform itself time and again even though the interior remains the same. Perhaps it's a tunnel to an extra-terrestrial space of ever-lasting youth?

127 CAFÉ AERA

Gonzagagasse 11
Innere Stadt ①
+43 (0)676 844 260 270
aera.at

The Aera is located in the former textile quarter of Vienna where there used to be plenty of Jewish shops. But it was also a nightlife district. Aera is one of the bars that lasted. You can have lunch or dinner at this cafe and they host all kinds of events at night.

128 CAFE KREUZBERG

Neustiftgasse 103
Neubau ⑤
+43 (0)699 114 947 33
kreuzberg.cc

Teeming with musicians. Music students from the nearby music school and many music professionals like to hang out at Café Kreuzberg. They love the informal, artistic atmosphere. There is a piano and if you are lucky one of the undiscovered talents will play a song for you. Party downstairs.

129 WERKZEUG H

**Schönbrunner-
strasse 61**
Margareten ④
+43 (0)1 913 87 28
werkzeugh.at

Werkzeug means tool. This place wants to be a tool, helping young people to meet, connect and share ideas. Also a good place for a cheap lunch, regardless of your age. Austrian and international cuisine, often curries. They also organise workshops, including a DIY dildo session.

130 DAS GAGARIN

Garnisongasse 24
Alsergrund ⑥
cafegagarin.at

Juri Alekseyevich Gagarin was a Russian cosmonaut and the first man in space. Das Gagarin is a collective, a new space where political discussions are welcome. And so are refugees too. You can eat lunch. Pay what you want. Be fair.

5

MUSIC CLUBS

you can't afford to miss

---

131 GRELLE FORELLE
Spittelauer Lände 12
Donaukanal ⑥
grelleforelle.com

The number one music club in town. Young people love it. They have several DJs but also live acts, including a collab with Indie radio station FM4. You sometimes have to queue. They do let people in that are 25 or older.

132 FLEX
Abgang
Augartenbrücke
Donaukanal ①
+43 (0)1 533 75 25
flex.at

The Flex is a classic. It was the first club on the banks of the Donaukanal. It still is everything. Now they have different floors and stages inside and outside. This is a rough place. At one time, it was the heart of Vienna's punk scene. Now there's just a general sense of nostalgia and graffiti wafting around.

133 PORGY & BESS
Riemergasse 11
Innere Stadt ①
+43 (0)1 512 88 11
porgy.at

Porgy & Bess is a jazz club. But it is also a place where creative people like to meet. They host world music, slam poetry and other events. They have lots of international collaborations, among others with Moods/Zurich, Jazzhouse/Copenhagen, Bimhuis/Amsterdam. Let them surprise you.

134 B72

**Hernalser
Gürtel 72-73
Josefstadt** ⑥
b72.at

Bogen means arch. And you can find this special music club at arch 72 along busy Hernalser Gürtel. It is oldie but goldie. They were one of the first clubs to bring interesting indie bands to Vienna. As the place is very small, you can get very close to the band.

135 RHIZ

**U-Bahnbogen 37
Josefstadt** ⑥
+43 (0)1 409 25 05
rhiz.org

Same same but different. Like B72 the Rhiz is located in a rough area under the metro arches. At one time, they were the only ones here but now there are several different bars so you can go on a pub crawl. Many live shows.

132 FLEX

5 places to
WALTZ

---

136 HOFBURG
Heldenplatz
Innere Stadt ①
+43 (0)1 587 36 66
hofburg.com

The Hofburg still is the most impressive imperial building in Vienna, and overlooks Heldenplatz. The best way of experiencing what life must have been like at the emperor's court is to attend a typical Viennese ball. There is a dress code. Women must wear a long evening dress while men should wear a Smoking, *Frack* or Uniform. It's like travelling back in time.

137 RATHAUS
Friedrich
Schmidt-Platz
Innere Stadt ①
+43 (0)1 400 00
wien.gv.at

The Rathaus, the city hall, is a beautiful building with its neo-Gothic towers and halls. Balls are much more informal here than in Hofburg. It hosts the AIDS Life Ball for example and many other balls, during which you can slip on your waltzing shoes. They also have a club where you can dance so don't be shy.

138 KONZERTHAUS

Lothringer-
strasse 20
Landstrasse ③
+43 (0)1 242 002
konzerthaus.at

Konzerthaus is a fantastic place to enjoy classical music. Some of the world's best musicians have given concerts here – but in wintertime you can also dance here. Check the programme for the list of traditional balls. Not as expensive as Hofburg but still very elegant.

139 PALAIS ESCHENBACH

Eschenbach-
gasse 9-11
Innere Stadt ①
+43 (0)699 196 817 02
palais-eschenbach.at

Emperor Franz Joseph I inaugurated the building in 1872. It is the perfect combination of old and new. Young people love it and often use it to celebrate their proms. There are many different balls here. Very informal, you can even wear a cocktail dress – as a man.

140 CASINO BAUMGARTEN

Linzer Strasse 297
Penzing ⑧⑪
+43 (0)1 236 52 89
casino-baumgarten.at

Casino Baumgarten was built as a castle for the noble Esterházy family in 1779 when this part of the city did not yet exist. It was transformed into a casino in the 19th century. Nowadays it's an elegant concert hall, which also hosts dancing events. A slice of history.

5 places to
DANCE THE LINDY HOP

---

141 SOME LIKE IT HOT BALLROOM
Sechshauser Strasse 9
Rudolfsheim-Fünfhaus ⑪
somelikeithot.at

Named after the famous film with Marilyn Monroe this ballroom is a classic. It is located in the basement of a turn of the century house. And nothing could prepare you for the splendid sight that awaits you. The walls are lined with mirrors, red velvet seats with golden chandeliers hanging from the ceiling.

142 CAFÉ FRANCAIS
Währinger Strasse 6-8
Alsergrund ⑥
+43 (0)1 319 09 03
cafefrancais.at

It's like Paris in Vienna. You can have a French breakfast, lunch or dinner – and you can even dance at night or just have a drink and watch other people dance in the basement. They have tango nights, but also Lindy Hop, catering to a young, fun crowd. No credit cards.

143 AZUL BAR
Postgasse 2
Innere Stadt ①
+43 (0)676 357 13 11
veranstaltungsraum.at

Azul means blue in Spanish. And this bar really makes you feel as you are in Spain or Latin America. It is quite accessible, and you soon feel as if you have already been here before. Have a drink and enjoy watching people dance in a familiar atmosphere.

144 25HOURS HOTEL DACHBODEN

Lerchenfelder
Strasse 1-3
Neubau ⑤
+43 (0)1 521 510
25hours-hotels.com

This could have also been included on the list of hipster places. The bar of the 25hours Hotel Neubau near MuseumsQuartier is a top location. It's open from 3 pm till 1 am and hosts plenty of different events including Swing 'n' Roll, Lindy Hop, Thirsty Thursday and many more. Very laidback.

145 EDISON

Alser Strasse 9
Josefstadt ⑥
+43 (0)1 236 33 18
edison.at

This used to be a music shop but now it's a cafe, a restaurant and a bar, on two floors. The name refers to a cafe Edison that opened here in 1922. The interior is quite cool, in a Scandi-kind of way. Famous for its cocktails.

THE LINDY HOP

The 5 best
PUBS

---

146 BOCKSHORN IRISH PUB

Naglergasse 7
Innere Stadt ①
+43 (0)1 532 94 38
bockshorn.at

Bockshorn is Vienna's oldest Irish Pub. It is located on narrow Naglergasse and it is tiny. They serve Newcastle Brown, Kilkenny, Murphy's, Stiegl, Hirter and of course Guinness. You can also enjoy Magners and Strongbow Cider here. Or sample one of 70 different whiskies. Check out their Malt Selection.

147 CHARLIE P'S PUB & KITCHEN

Währinger Strasse 3
Alsergrund ⑥
+43 (0)1 409 79 23
charlieps.at

Students love this place. This pub has everything a pub needs, including different beers and sports as well as a downstairs. In this case that means Monday Rock n' Roll Karaoke, Tuesday is Medical Tuesday with hundreds of soon to be doctors partying. Don't miss Thursday: Bad Taste Night.

148 FLANAGANS IRISH PUB VIENNA

Schwarzenberg-
strasse 1-3
Innere Stadt ①
flanagans.at

Expats love Flanagans. If you like a place with international flair, then come to this large Irish Pub. There's always a table on either of the two floors even when it's crowded – and it always is. Very friendly staff, good burgers. Sports on the telly. This place is so great that it doesn't matter that their webpage is not mobile-friendly.

149 O'CONNOR'S OLD OAK

Rennweg 95
Landstrasse ③
oconnors.at

This pub in Vienna's 3rd district is run by two Irish brothers. They cook up and serve good pub grub here and have an excellent drinks selection. The menu features starters and snacks, salads and sandwiches, steaks and spare ribs. Try the chocolate brownie or their sticky toffee pudding.

150 JOHNNY'S PUB

Schleifmühlgasse 11
Naschmarkt ④
+43 (0)1 587 19 21
johnnys-pub.at

Johnny's is located in vibrant Schleif-mühlgasse. This pub and party venue hosts different live gigs and has a friendly, lively atmosphere. You can eat, drink, chill out or party till late: Sunday and Monday from 5 pm till 2 am, and Tuesday till Saturday from 5 pm till 4 am.

5 spots
BARISTAS
love

---

151 KOFFEINSCHMIEDE
Schimmelgasse 12
Landstrasse ③
koffeinschmiede.at

All in one: the best coffees from Panama, single origin, 100% arabica, bought directly from the growers. They also sell coffee machines and equipment and offer barista workshops. They founded Baristas United, a community for baristas. A place for specialists.

152 BARISTAS UNITED
Schrottgasse 7
Landstrasse ③
+43 (0)1 714 187 912
baristasunited.at

At Baristas United they sell Sanremo coffee makers: *Opera* is the queen and *Café Racer* is the king. They have a showroom, repair and assembly shop. Very slick, very fashionable.

153 ALT WIEN KAFFEE
Schleifmühlgasse 23
Naschmarkt ④
+43 (0)1 505 08 00
altwien.at

The Alt Wien Kaffee was one of the first of its kind in Vienna. Christian Schrödl opened it before the coffee hype. In 2008 Oliver Goetz, a regular, joined him. Since then they have continued to sell quality organic, fair trade and Demeter coffee. Simply the best.

154 KAFFEEFABRIK
Favoritenstrasse 4-6
Wieden ④
+43 (0)660 178 90 92
kaffeefabrik.at

Kaffeefabrik is a coffee bar and roastery, so two for the price of one. They have a very strict policy: all their coffee is sourced directly from the growers in northern Nicaragua and SHG (strictly high grown above 1100 metres). Try this special '*Grandoro*'!

155 WOLFGANG COFFEE
Zieglergasse 38
Neubau ⑤
+43 (0)650 220 03 80
dieparfumerie.net

You can find Wolfgang Coffee in a QWSTION Store. After shopping you can sip a homemade Espresso Roast 'Leitwolf', which means Alphawoolf. The coffee is roasted by Wildkaffee in Garmisch-Partenkirchen, which really is in the woods. If you are not that wild, then give 'Wolfshund' from Süssmund a try.

153 ALT WIEN KAFFEE

65 PLACES
TO SHOP

---

5 shops for
BITS & BOBS

---

156 FREDERIK'S

Taborstrasse 24-A
Leopoldstadt ②
+43 (0)1 214 99 99
frederiks.at

Frederik's is a well-known high-class caterer in Vienna, but it also is a shop where you can find plenty of beautiful things for cooking and living. Gourmet essentials, books, accessories, tableware, interior decoration by different young artists in a pop-up concept. Everything you don't really need but would love to have.

157 STATTGARTEN SHOP

Kettenbrücken-
gasse 14
Naschmarkt ④
+43 (0)1 236 35 93
stattgarten.wien

Pasta and brooms. Harry Potter would really love this shop! Once again, Christian Jauernik managed to create something truly special. The creative consultant and his wife Eva Seisser already run an excellent natural cosmetic shop. This time around, they chose to combine a selection of quality food and homewares.

158 LA SCHACHTULA

Kettenbrücken-
gasse 6
Naschmarkt ④
+43 (0)1 890 31 84
laschachtula.at

La Schachtula only uses Austrian textiles from the Mühlviertel and the Waldviertel for its textiles for the kitchen, bathroom and children. Everything is handmade in Austria. A good place to shop for a newborn.

159 **ANNA STEIN SALON**

Kettenbrücken-
gasse 21
Naschmarkt ④
+43 (0)699 120 314 30
anna-stein.com

Anna Stein Salon is named after its owner and sells a nice selection of accessories for the home and living as well as jewellery and handmade scarves. Every single thing in the shop has a story. Let Anna tell you all about it.

160 **WIENER SEIFE**

Hintzerstrasse 6
Landstrasse ③
+43 (0)1 715 31 71
wienerseife.at

They only sell soap here but it's a very special one. The *rezepture* is a well-kept secret. They use the best natural oils, extracts and perfumes for their hand-made products. Try Bergamotte N° 57 or one of the other retro style soaps. A great alternative to the usual souvenirs from Vienna.

5

MUSEUM SHOPS
you should definitely check out

---

161 MAK

Stubenring 5
Innere Stadt ①
+43 (0)1 711 360
mak.at

The MAK, *Museum für angwandte Kunst*, is Vienna's museum of applied arts. Visit the spacious shop. Tableware, books, bags… Here you can find gifts for your friends and family. They have the usual Klimt leporello, as well as more unique treasures. A must-see for architecture lovers.

162 KUNST-HISTORISCHES MUSEUM

Maria-Theresien Platz
Innere Stadt ①
+43 (0)1 525 243 300
khm.at

The Kunsthistorisches Museum is Vienna's most important museum, showcasing 125 years of history, so don't miss the collection before you head to the shop. Explore Brueghel under a microscope or come eye to eye with Klimt. Then select your favourite pictures as postcards.

163 WELTMUSEUM ✓

Heldenplatz
Innere Stadt ①
+43 (0)1 534 305 052
weltmuseumwien.at

The Quetzal feather headdress is the most important piece in the collection of the newly-laid out Weltmuseum (former museum of popular art), an ethnological museum in beautiful Hofburg. See items from around the world, buy the Weltmuseum memory game and check whether you can remember them all.

164 MUMOK ✓

Museumsplatz 1
MuseumsQuartier ⑤
+43 (0)1 525 000
mumok.at

The mumok is Vienna's museum of modern art. It may not be as famous as the one in New York but it is the best we have. The collection focusses on the Wiener Gruppe. The architecture (by Ortner & Ortner) is also worth seeing. Buy a unique print from mumok editions.

165 JÜDISCHES MUSEUM WIEN

Dorotheergasse 11
Innere Stadt ①
+43 (0)1 535 04 31
jmw.at

Vienna's Jewish museum is located in two different locations. Start by visiting the British artist Rachel Whiteread's Holocaust Memorial in Judenplatz, then see different exhibitions about Helena Rubinstein or Teddy Kollek for example in Dorotheergasse. The museum has a small, but well-stocked shop.

5 great places to
BUY ART

---

166 GEORG KARGL GALLERY

Schleifmühlgasse 5
Wieden ④
+43 (0)1 585 41 99
georgkargl.com

Schleifmühlgasse is still the most important address in Vienna for modern art. In 1998, Georg Kargl opened his Fine Arts Gallery with an exhibition space of more than 300 square metres on three floors. Georg Kargl passed away in 2018 but his mission of hosting exhibitions and promoting emerging artist will live on.

167 KERSTIN ENGHOLM GALLERY

Schleifmühlgasse 3
Wieden ④
+43 (0)1 585 73 37
kerstinengholm.com

One year after the Georg Kargl Gallery, Kerstin Engholm Gallery opened next door. Engholm has focussed on the exchange between young Austrian and international artists from the start. Come on Thursday evenings during the opening of the Galerienrundgang.

168 GALERIE CHRISTINE KÖNIG

Schleifmühlgasse 1-A
Wieden ④
+43 (0)1 585 74 74
christine
koeniggalerie.com

The third of the three Schleifmühlgassen galleries is Galerie Christine König. Christine König moved her existing gallery to Schleifmühlgasse in 1999. She focusses on politics and activism, feminism and literature. Young artists welcome!

169 GALERIE URSULA KRINZINGER ✓

Seilerstätte 16
Innere Stadt ①
+43 (0)1 513 30 06
galerie-krinzinger.at

Ursula Krinzinger is the Grande Dame of Vienna's modern art scene. Her gallery was there before the stars of Schleifmühlgasse burst onto the scene. She started out 40 years ago. Discover a selection of 118 posters, 332 contemporary art books and 70 multiples in her shop.

170 ART FOUNDATION

Schadekgasse 6-8
Mariahilf ⑤
+43 (0)699 152 313 49
artfoundation.at

Art Foundation is a multi-space organisation. Here you'll find Amer Abas with his Kunstbüro Gallery in Schadekgasse, Büro Weltausstellung in Praterstrasse 42(1/3) and Kunstraum am Schauplatz, also located at Praterstrasse 42. Rely on Amer's expertise if you are interested in buying work by young artists.

168 GALERIE CHRISTINE KÖNIG

The 5 best
BAKERIES

---

171 GRAGGER

Vorgartenmarkt
Stand 14-15
Leopoldstadt ②
+43 (0)1 664 413 72 77
gragger.at

Vorgartenmarkt is one of Vienna's upcoming farmer's markets and Gragger bakery helped transform it into what it is today. Here you can buy organic bread but the bakery itself is also Insta-worthy. They bake their bread in a wood oven and have three tables if you want to sample the goods on the spot.

171 GRAGGER

172 WALDHERR

Marc-Aurel-Strasse 4
Innere Stadt ①
+43 (0)2 682 610 08
*vollkornbaeckerei-
waldherr.at*

Your go-to baker if you have a gluten intolerance, allergy or something else. Waldherr bakes sour dough bread with old grains, like spelt, rye or amaranth. They also have a gluten-free rice bread. Vegans love it. What's more, his bread is all fair trade.

173 ANKERBROT

Absberggasse 35
Favoriten ⑨
ankerbrot.at

Ankerbrot is a classic. They've been in business for 125 years. In 1891, Heinrich and Fritz Mendel founded the company that has been supplying bread to the royal household since 1901. After the aryanisation during World War II, the family got their company back after the war. Still yummy.

174 JOSEPH BROT

Landstrasser
Hauptstrasse 4
Landstrasse ③
+43 (0)1 710 28 81
joseph.co.at

Joseph Brot is the most famous baker in Vienna. Josef Weghaupt was one of the first bakers to launch a new baking tradition in 2009 when the market was mostly inundated with industrial bread. He recreated old recipes and (re-)introduced the city to quality bread. Now there are four shops, in Landstrasse you can also stop for a snack.

175 BÄCKEREI CAFÉ FELZL

Lerchenfelder
Strasse 99-101
Neubau ⑤
+43 (0)1 522 38 09
felzl.at

Felzl is completely bobo (short for 'bourgeois bohemian'). They sell delicious organic bread but it's an exercise in patience as there's always a queue. Great people watching here.

5 of the sweetest
CHOCOLATE SHOPS

176 XOCOLAT

Freyung 2
Innere Stadt ①
+43 (0)1 535 43 63
xocolat.at

There are many chocolate shops in Vienna but Xocolat is the most spectacular. Situated in beautiful Palais Ferstel, which was used as the former national bank from 1855 onwards, this is one of the shops in Ferstel Passage. Here you can combine fine architecture with exquisite chocolate.

177 SCHOKOV

Siebensterngasse 20
Neubau ⑤
+43 (0)680 300 08 60
schokov.com

Extraordinary chocolates for extraordinary people. In 2006 the former copywriter Thomas 'tomkov' Kovazh decided to realise his dream of making people happy with chocolate. Since then he has won various international awards. All fair trade and handmade.

178 LESCHANZ

Mollardgasse 85-A
Naschmarkt ④
+43 (0)1 596 78 77
leschanz.at

This place is all about family and tradition. Leschanz is the king of chocolate which is why he wears a crown in his logo. Here you buy traditional seasonal chocolate sweets for Easter or Christmas, which are all handmade of course. Maybe not the most experimental chocolatier, but great attention to detail.

179 SCHOKO COMPANY

Naschmarkt
Stand 326-331
Naschmarkt ④
+43 (0)660 688 24 88
schokocompany.at

Schoko Company is a paradise. Here you find all kinds of chocolate from Steiermark, in the south of Austria where the famous Zotter Schokolade comes from. Zotter was one of the first to experiment with special flavours such as pumpkin seed. They also have a snack bar.

180 BONBONS

Neubaugasse 18
Neubau ⑤
+43 (0)1 523 63 60
*bonbons-
neubaugasse.at*

Bonbons is a traditional Viennese *Zuckerlgeschäft* where you can buy chocolate and candy. It was there before the chocolate hype and it will still be there when it's over. It is so old-fashioned that it has become hip again. Come and sample some *Krachmandeln* or *Seidenzuckerln.*

The 5 finest
TEA SHOPS

---

181 SCHÖNBICHLER

Wollzeile 4
Innere Stadt ①
+43 (0)1 512 18 16
teegschwendner.at

Theehandlung Schönbichler (they spell it like that) is a magnificent shop in Wollzeile where the rich people always used to shop specialities from all over the world. They sell black and green tea, white tea, ayurvedic and seasonal teas as well as spirits from Destillerie Freihof.

182 DEMMERS TEEHAUS

Mölker Bastei 5
Innere Stadt ①
+43 (0)1 533 59 95
tee.at

Demmers Teehaus has various shops around Vienna, but we prefer the one at Mölker Bastei because of their impressive tea selection. Try their tea sampler from different countries and choose your favourite.

183 SIR HARLY'S TEA

Raimundhof
Mariahilf ⑤
+43 (0)660 777 19 99
harly-tea.at

Sir Harly's Tea is tucked away in Raimundhof, a silent refuge near busy Mariahilfer Strasse. Their philosophy is to not stock too much, but always make sure everything is fresh. Come in the afternoon to enjoy Five O'Clock tea with pastries, sandwiches or scones with clotted cream. Very British!

184 JÄGER TEE

Operngasse 6
Innere Stadt ①
+43 (0)1 512 62 59
jaegertee.at

Even window shopping is fun here. Jäger Tee is Vienna's oldest shop (1892), specialising in tea from Asia. They have such beautiful tea pots as well as Buddhas of all kinds and sizes. Try one of their teas in their Japanese tearoom.

185 HAAS & HAAS

Stephansplatz 4
Innere Stadt ①
+43 (0)1 512 26 66
haas-haas.at

The architecture is just one of the reasons why you should visit this place. Haas & Haas is situated in an historic building opposite Stephansdom, one of the town's landmarks. They have extended their range in recent years with teas, marmalades, chocolates and even coffee.

181 SCHÖNBICHLER

5
FARMER'S MARKETS
you shouldn't miss

186 KARMELITERMARKT

Karmeliterplatz
Leopoldstadt ②
stadt-wien.at/
wien/maerkte/
karmelitermarkt.html

Karmelitermarkt is simply the best. It opened in 1891 but was destroyed during World War II. It became cool again around the year 2000. Since 2008, there is a special slow food area here. Visit on Saturdays when the local farmers sell their produce here until 1 pm.

189 BRUNNENMARKT

187 VORGARTENMARKT

Vorgartenplatz
Leopoldstadt ②
vorgartenmarkt.at

A new metro line (number two) has accelerated the gentrification of the neighbourhood near Prater, which used to be the city's red-light district. Now Stuwerviertel is a popular quarter after Vienna's new business university was built here. A great place for organic produce as well as meat and bread.

188 NASCHMARKT

Naschmarkt
Naschmarkt ④
*wien.gv.at/freizeit/
einkaufen/maerkte/
lebensmittel/
naschmarkt/
details.html*

Naschmarkt is one of the oldest markets in Vienna (since 1786), and the biggest. There are 123 stalls in this 2,3 hectare market. The market square was designed by the famous architect Otto Wagner in 1916. It is not actually a square but a lane where you buy all kinds of artisan delicacies.

189 BRUNNENMARKT

Brunnengasse
Ottakring ⑪
*stadt-wien.at/
wien/maerkte/
brunnenmarkt.html*

Some people call it little Istanbul. Brunnenmarkt is a mainly Turkish market, but you can also buy Arab specialities here. Don't be shy! The ever-crowded and vibrant market invites visitors to enjoy lunch on the go. Have a fresh *kebab* and some *chai*.

190 KUTSCHKERMARKT

Kutschkergasse
Währing ⑪
*amkutschker
markt.at*

This small, but very beautiful market is named after Johann Rudolf Kutschker, a liberal bishop. It was first referenced in 1885 when it started around St. Gertruds Church. Today it is the heart of this bourgeois neighbourhood. Here you can find locally-sourced ingredients, cheese and flowers.

The 5 best
BIKE SHOPS

---

191 VELETAGE

Praterstrasse 13
Leopoldstadt ②
+43 (0)1 212 49 11
veletage.com

Bike repairs are their daily bread. At Veletage, *Salon für Radkultur*, a bike is like an artwork culture. So they produce your handmade bespoke bike especially for you and your needs. They have a selection of bike gear, including some brands for women only, which is quite rare.

192 COOPERATIVE FAHRRAD

Gumpendorfer
Strasse 87
Mariahilf ⑤
+43 (0)1 596 52 56
fahrrad.co.at

For over 30 years, Cooperative Fahrrad has been selling high-quality bikes in Vienna. Their range includes city and travel bikes, bicycle trailers and accessories of all kinds. They sell e-bikes and are the leading dealer for Brompton (smart folding bike) in Austria.

193 ROADBIKER

Praterstrasse 29
Leopoldstadt ②
+43 (0)1 264 53 81
mountainbiker.at

Roadbiker is kind of an allrounder. They sell city bikes, racing bikes and mountain bikes. They have a much bigger selection than Veletage, but it is not that high end. You don't have to be a pro to shop here. Very nice and excellent sales advice if you need a helmet.

194 REANIMATED-BIKES

Westbahnstrasse 35
Neubau ⑤
+43 (0)1 522 40 18
reanimated-bikes.com

Upcycling is a hot topic in many fields – including in the bike industry. Reanimated-Bikes makes your old bike all brand new. They focus on city bikes and are proof that you can also use a mountain bike for your daily commute. Try them out!

195 RIH

Praterstrasse 48
Leopoldstadt ②
+43 (0)1 214 51 80
m.radsport-rih.com

Rih is not so fancy – but it is all about tradition here. The shop was founded in 1933 by Franz Hamedl sen, who co-founded the Tour of Austria. Still the best place for racing pros. These experts sell for top-quality bikes for top-quality cyclists. Not for everyday bikes.

5 of the sweetest
CANDY SHOPS

---

196 ZUCKERL-WERKSTATT

Herrengasse 6-8
Innere Stadt ①
+43 (0)1 890 90 56
zuckerlwerkstatt.at

Handmade moments of happiness. At Zuckerlwerkstatt, they relied on old recipes for the formulation of their 90 different flavours. If you are planning a special event or are looking for a fun give-away for your company, then have them print your logo on their candy.

197 SNACK SHOP

Liechtenstein-strasse 25
Alsergrund ⑥
+43 (0)1 317 25 79
snackshop.at

Snacks, sweets and soft drinks… It's all about quantity here. If you are in search of sweets that you can't usually find in Austria, then look no further. Fluffy marshmallow strawberries or double dipped nerd's lemonade with wild cherry apple watermelon. Trick-or-treat all year long.

198 BOBBY'S FOODSTORE

Schleifmühlgasse 8
Naschmarkt ④
+43 (0)1 586 75 34
bobbys.at

Expats love this food shop. Here you can buy British and American food and sweets. If you feel a little homesick as a visitor, then pop in here and bag yourself some biscuits, pudding, candy and crisps. Bobby's has the most excellent stock. He was the first and is still the best.

199 **NOBNOBS**

Neubaugasse 80
Neubau ⑤
+43 (0)676 922 78 71
nobnobs.at

Handmade candy always tastes good but did you know it tastes even better when you make it yourself? In Neubaugasse, you can enjoy quite a show. Four times a day you can see the team at work, producing new candy. Have you run out of ideas for a birthday party? Then book a workshop for your child and his or her friends. Just as much fun without children.

200 **ZUCKERLTANTE**

Klosterneuburger
Strasse 30
Brigittenau ⑦
+43 (0)1 330 31 21

Old but fun. The owner Monika Erhart is so old-fashioned that she doesn't believe in the need of such thing as a website. There are so many regulars who love Zuckerltante that she just keeps on selling her old-fashioned candy. It's like travelling back in time to your childhood.

199 NOBNOBS

5
CONCEPT STORES
worth a visit

---

201 STRICTLY HERRMANN

Taborstrasse 5
Leopoldstadt ②
+43 (0)1 997 27 57
strictlyherrmann.com

Strictly Hermann is a concept store that is strictly for men only, selling gadgets, selected fashions, watches, perfumes, books and gin. You can also book the shop for a business event. Recently, the creative director Philipp Bruni and owner Claudia Rauhofer opened an art gallery downstairs. Women welcome.

202 WUNDERTÜTE

Karmeliterplatz 2
Leopoldstadt ②
+43 (0)664 283 55 46
wundertuete.at

Wundertüte means grab bag. Although in this case, it's more of a goodie bag with accessories, jewellery, bags, books, body creams, green tea and artisan delicacies. And Austrian fashion by well- or less well-known labels. Every single piece is personally selected by the shop's owner Petra Raab. A real trend scout – get to know her.

203 PREGENZER

Schleifmühlgasse 4
Naschmarkt ④
+43 (0)1 586 57 58
pregenzer.com

Fashion, shoes, flowers, jewellery and books. The shop is a world unto its own – the world of owner Jutta Pregenzer and her passion for details and only the highest quality. Her purist *pot-pourrie* is a must see for any stylish woman. You can request a personal appointment.

204 DER AFFE UND DER BRÄUTIGAM

Grosse Sperlgasse 8
Leopoldstadt ②
+43 (0)1 958 10 74
derkleinesalon.at

Der Affe und der Bräutigam is a play by the famous writer Johann Nestroy, who wrote it for an actor who was living in the house where you can find this concept store for the whole family. Verena Wibmer-Oppolzer and Carolin Rukschcio select wall stickers, tablecloths, wooden toys, shoes and fashion – with love!

205 LUV THE SHOP

Taborstrasse 24
Leopoldstadt ②
+43 (0)1 958 04 32
luvtheshop.com

Storytelling is second nature to them. The owners Karin and Leena love Scandi design and the Nordic laidback, unfussy attitude: find Selected Femme, Yaya, Cowboysbag and many more must-brands. For urban hipsters!

202 WUNDERTÜTE

5 of the best
BOOKSHOPS

---

206 LHOTZKYS LITERATURBUFFET

Rotensterngasse 2
Leopoldstadt ②
+43 (0)1 276 47 36
literaturbuffet.com

Anyone who is interested in politics, history and the local history of Vienna should head to Lhotzkys Literaturbuffet. Kurt Lhotzky runs it with his family. Here you can meet, enjoy a snack or a chat, with other patrons or even Kurt himself. His knowledge about history, especially Marxism and Jewish culture, is simply astonishing.

207 TIEMPO NUEVO

Taborstrasse 17-A
Leopoldstadt ②
+43 (0)1 908 13 26
tiempo.at

A great place for open-minded people or globetrotters. They sell books from around the world with an emphasis on the Middle East and the Orient. A good selection of English books, and they also host interesting talks.

208 A.PUNKT

Fischerstiege 1-7
Innere Stadt ①
+43 (0)1 532 85 14
apunktbuch.at

Brigitte Salanda, the owner, is a Viennese original. She's been in the business for over 50 years. She specialises in psychoanalysis, but she's also always up for a chat about the latest publications. That is, if she's interested in it. A very small and special place. Stay away if you're looking for more random stuff.

209 BUCHHANDLUNG WALTHER KÖNIG

Museumsplatz 1-A
MuseumsQuartier ⑤
+43 (0)1 512 858 80
mqw.at

This place has an amazing selection of coffee table books about architecture, design and arts as well as special publications for academic readers. Visiting this shop in fancy MuseumsQuartier is a bit like a social safari. You'll bump into architects and art students.

210 LIA WOLF CABINETT

Sonnenfelsgasse 3
Innere Stadt ①
+43 (0)1 512 40 94
wolf.at

Lia Wolf's bookstore is not just a shop – it's a *Cabinett*, a microcosmos in the heart of the old city. She has created a Wunderkammer full of books about art, design, architecture and graphics in an old building. She often organises exhibitions and talks – in summer in the beautiful backyard, in winter in the reading room.

210 LIA WOLF CABINETT

5 *for*
SPECIAL INTEREST

211 PARFUMERIE J.B. FILZ

Graben 13
Innere Stadt ①
+43 (0)1 512 17 45
parfumerie-filz.at

Being extraordinary has been their business premise since 1809. They endeavour to find only the best products for your body, hair and *maquillage* as they call it. This perfumery in Vienna's Graben, a pedestrian zone and elegant promenade, still has the same flair it had under the monarchy.

212 KNIZE

Graben 13
Innere Stadt ①
+43 (0)1 512 21 19
knize.at

This famous tailor has always had a very demanding clientele, including the emperor himself and several other scions of the Habsburg family. They have been providing the finest bespoke suits here since 1858. In the twenties, Ernst Dryden transformed Knize into one of the first labels of modern times.

213 KUSSMUND

Habsburgergasse 14
Innere Stadt ①
+43 (0)1 535 51 95
kussmund.wien

Natural cosmetics, special luxury perfumes and fancy make up. This shop specialises in the little luxurious of life, including scented candles, bath oils and pretty accessories. It's easy to find too: look for the kissing lips logo.

214 AUGARTEN FLAGSHIPSTORE

Spiegelgasse 3
Innere Stadt ①
+43 (0)1 512 14 94
augarten.com

The famous porcelain manufactory in Augarten was founded over 300 years ago. Since its inception, Augarten has always worked closely with contemporary artists. Its 'Vogelkolonie' (white and black swans) teapot by Koloman Moser is just one of many classics you can buy here, as well as tablewares, figurines and gifts.

215 LIEBENSWERT

Esterhazygasse 26
Mariahilf ⑤
+43 (0)1 595 52 55
liebens-wert.at

Liebenswert is a sex shop – but not your usual kind. The owner Ingrid Mack wanted to create a space especially for women to discover their erotic needs or dreams. So here you'll be advised by women. Check out the website for the tip of the month.

214 AUGARTEN FLAGSHIPSTORE

5 *for*
KNITTING

---

216 WOLLMEILE

Taborstrasse 24-A
Leopoldstadt ②
+43 (0)1 968 54 24
wollmeile.at

First New York, then Berlin and two years later Vienna. That's the way things go in fashion, as well as in knitting. Which is why knitting is still all the rage in Vienna. Wollmeile is still one of the nicest wool shops in town. Every Wednesday there is an open knitting group from 5.30 pm till 8 pm.

217 WOLLEWIEN

Fleischmarkt 13
Innere Stadt ①
+43 (0)1 532 03 98
wollewien.at

WolleWien is very popular for its yarns, like organic bamboo, recycled cotton and cork yarn. They have a magnificent selection of soft merinos in plenty of colours and four different weights. The only place in Vienna to sell the full range of The Fibre Company.

218 WEDERMANN

Mariahilfer
Strasse 101
Mariahilf ⑤
+43 (0)1 596 51 25
wedermann.co.at

The experts for all things felt and wool. You'll find this speciality shop on Vienna's largest shopping boulevard. They buy and sell knitting machines and do have the know-how to repair your knitting machine even when it's very old.

219 PINGOUIN WOLLBOUTIQUE

Alserstrasse 21
Alsergrund ⑥
+43 (0)1 408 00 10
pingouinwolle.at

Get your wool fix in this tiny shop, which has the biggest selection. The Pingouin Wollboutique opened its doors in 1985, so it was there before the big knitting hype and it will still be there when the hype is over. The official Lana Grossa store is a must see for all knitting fans.

220 WIENER WOLLCAFÉ

Beatrixgasse 4
Landstrasse ③
+43 (0)699 152 499 11
laniato.com

Happiness is handmade. Topsy Thun-Hohenstein believes in the force of knitting. You can even knit on hot summer days, switching to mohair seta, crochet yarn, lightly-plied cotton and more. There is no such thing as an off-season in knitting. Sit down at the large table and have a coffee.

SONG

55 PLACES FOR FASHION & DESIGN

The 5 best places for
JEWELLERY

---

221 MOHA

Koellnerhofgasse 3
Innere Stadt ①
+43 (0)676 400 77 04
moha.at

Franz Motoch's shop is like a gallery for contemporary jewellery. He provides a platform for young designers. Here you'll find the unusual, rather than the usual. He also is a strong believer in fair trade gold. Eppi Nölke, Nicole Wagner, Nicole Eitel and Oliver Schmidt only work with this type of gold, which is imported from Argentina.

222 NEUNER SCHMUCK ATELIER

KärntnerStrasse 8
Innere Stadt ①
+43 (0)1 907 66 43
aljaandfriends.com

Are you looking for a special gift for a dear friend? Then check out Neuner Schmuck Atelier at Alja & Friends. This place is a studio, a gallery and a designer's workshop. Its concrete window displays are quite remarkable. Go see upstairs how the jewellery is produced.

223 KATIE G. JEWELLERY

Lindengasse 5
Neubau ⑤
+43 (0)681 207 193 92
katiegruber.com

Turn an old ring into a new one. Katie had the idea when she became engaged and was given a solitaire, which was a family heirloom. She created a new ring that respects the integrity of the original and specialises in this patented design. Bring in an old ring or have Katie design you a new one.

224 ATELIER STOSS IM HIMMEL

Stoss im Himmel 3
Innere Stadt ①
+43 (0)650 200 32 79
stossimhimmel.net

The eight members of a collective all stick to their own concept and material experiments, creating eight unique and individual visions on jewellery. If you have always wanted to create your own unique piece, for your wedding for example, then you have come to the right place. You can also take workshops here.

225 RINGKING

Kleeblattgasse 9
Innere Stadt ①
+43 (0)699 173 411 44
ring-king.com

Max Grün is the king of rings. He loves animals, so sells a monkey ring in pink gold as well as a duck ring in yellow gold. You can also add diamonds to sparkle up any occasion. Grün's eye-catching, loud and fun jewellery is definitely not for shy wallflowers.

5 interesting places for
VINTAGE

226 HUMANA

Taborstrasse 20-A
Leopoldstadt ②
+43 (0)1 212 45 29
humana.at

Humana is a nonprofit organisation that runs twelve secondhand shops in Vienna which sell very affordable items. Our favourite is the one in Taborstrasse. Not the biggest one perhaps but the one with the politest service. What's more, you support NGO projects in Africa when you shop at Humana.

227 BOCCALUPO

Landskrongasse 1-3
Innere Stadt ①
+43 (0)1 532 49 93
boccalupo.at

Boccalupo is Italian for good luck. If you are searching for luxury secondhand bags, accessories, shoes and fashion, you'll find all this and plenty more here. They only sell items with the right logo of course, like Chanel, Valentino, Prada. Boccalupo applies a strict no-fake-policy and collaborates with the labels to ensure no fakes are sold.

227 BOCCALUPO

228 BOOTIK 54

Neubaugasse 54
Neubau ⑤
bootik54.com

Bootik 54 has become so successful that they now have two little shops side by side. It is situated in fashionable Neubaugasse. Not exactly cheap and plenty of fancy options. For men and women, although who cares about this distinction in the era of unisex. As you can tell from their name, they also sell boots and shoes.

229 UPPERS AND DOWNERS

Burggasse 46
Neubau ⑤
+43 (0)650 990 08 22
uppersand
downers.com

'You are a fucking lady.' I think this shop's motto says it all. Don't care what others think of you, stand by your own choices. You can combine all the clothes and accessories whichever way you want. And no, they don't sell pills here.

230 DAS NEUE SCHWARZ

Landskrongasse 1
Innere Stadt ①
+43 (0)1 532 01 05
dasneueschwarz.at

Das Neue Schwarz has been called Berlin's best vintage store. Now they have a branch in Vienna. Das Neue Schwarz means the new black – whichever is the new black this season. Depends on your cup of tea. Their community is impressive. Lots of influencers.

5 of the best
SHOE SHOPS

---

231 SHU!
Neubaugasse 34
Neubau ⑤
+43 (0)1 523 14 49
shu.at

If you visit Concept Store Park, then follow up with a visit to this shop on the opposite side of the street. The perfect place if you're looking for something special. Extraordinary men's and women's shoes. Closed on Mondays.

232 FOOTSTEPS
Fleischmarkt 12-A
Innere Stadt ①
+43 (0)1 513 73 77
footsteps.at

This shop is all about trainers. Look for the large window displays in a lovely fin de siècle building to get an idea of what awaits inside. Then pop in and buy, buy, buy. Very friendly staff.

233 LUDWIG REITER
Mölker Steig 1
Innere Stadt ①
+43 (0)1 533 42 04
ludwig-reiter.com

Ludwig Reiter sells shoes, rather than trainers. In 1885, Ludwig Reiter I moved to Vienna from Bohemia where he opened a shoemaker's. Ludwig Reiter II travelled to America where he learnt all kinds of new techniques, while the third generation focussed on custom-made shoes. And that is what the fourth generation Ludwig Reiter is known for today, namely the same reputable quality.

234 GEA

Lange Gasse 24
Josefstadt ⑥
+43 (0)1 408 36 26
gea-waldviertler.at

Heini Staudinger travelled around Africa during his studies, which proved a life-changing experience. He dropped out of medical school, hitchhiking to Denmark to find some special shoes. Then he developed his own company called Gea. The Waldviertler shoes are from northeast Austria. Handmade, functional and last forever.

235 HOUSE OF DANCING

Jörgerstrasse 34
Hernals ⑪
+43 (0)1 403 72 45
houseofdancing.com

Do you love to dance? Good. If you didn't until now, then Vienna might make you change your mind. There are so many different dancing events and classes, including modern, traditional, Latin, waltz. And there are different types of shoes for all these styles of dance. The experts at the House of Dancing will help you find the right one.

5 places to
PUT A HAT ON

236 MÜHLBAUER HUTMANUFAKTUR

Neubaugasse 34
Neubau ⑤
+43 (0)1 890 32 95
muehlbauer.at

Fifteen years ago, many people thought that hatmaking was a dying trade but Klaus Mühlbauer is living proof that the opposite is true. His family has been in the hatmaking business since 1903 and he is leading it to new heights. Mühlbauer hats are worn all around the world, including in Japan.

236 MÜHLBAUER HUTMANUFAKTUR

237 GESCHWISTER MAUERER

Mariahilfer
Strasse 117
Mariahilf ⑤
+43 (0)1 587 40 73
hut.co.at

Mauerer was established in 1873. Go to the main shop in Mariahilfer Strasse, which is definitely worth seeing it. The old façade is painted a bright poppy red. Here you'll find classics such as Borsalino and Stetson and their own creations. For men and women.

238 NAGY HÜTE WIEN

Wollzeile 36
Innere Stadt ①
+43 (0)1 405 66 29 21
m.nagy-hut.at

Nagy is one of the most traditional hat shops in Vienna. The name is originally Hungarian and the pronunciation does not resemble the spelling in any way. Even the locals have no idea how to pronounce it. But who cares? Pop in, and have the friendly staff find the right hat for you.

239 VIKTORYAS HUTSALON

Josefstädter-
strasse 38
Josefstadt ⑥
+43 (0)699 121 566 34
hutsalon.at

Were you invited to a wedding and don't know what to wear? Score a new fascinator to add a touch of glamour to an old dress. Even better, you can also find a new dress here. At Victoryas Hutsalon, they have the right outfit for every occasion.

240 HATTITUDE
AT: SCHNITTBOGEN

U-Bahn Bogen 3-4
Gumpendorfer
Gürtel
Mariahilf ⑤
+43 (0)680 401 67 12
schnittbogen.at

Hattitude is a combination of hat and attitude. Christina Lichy is a young Danish designer and hatmaker, who is inspired by long walks in nature, in the zoo and by films from the fifties. And now you can find her hats, caps and turbans at Schnittbogen in Vienna.

5
UPCOMING LABELS
in Vienna

---

241 PITOUR

Museumsplatz 1
MuseumsQuartier ⑤
+43 (0)699 120 089 20
pitour.com

Maria Oberfrank is the mastermind and the one-woman-show behind Pitour. She designs fashion for men and women, striking a nice balance between trends and pure elegance. Her designs can be worn for work or parties. Every item in her collection is timeless.

242 ARTISTA

Museumsplatz 1
MuseumsQuartier ⑤
+43 (0)1 236 05 96
artistafashion.com

Artista is a ready-to-wear-label. It was founded in Budapest by Katalin Imre, Nóra Rácz and Katalin Stampf. In Vienna you can find their designs at Combinat in MuseumsQuartier (together with Pitour) or at the MQ Vienna Fashionweek.

241 **PITOUR**

243 ELFENKLEID

Margareten-
strasse 39
Margareten ④
+43 (0)1 208 52 41
elfenkleid.com

Elfenkleid are famous for their wedding dresses. They offer made-to-measure and ready-made-dresses. If you want to be a modern bride, then have them help you find the right model. If you just need an elegant cocktail dress, then pop in and choose it yourself.

244 ART UP

Bauernmarkt 8
Innere Stadt ①
+43 (0)1 535 50 97
artup.at

Milch is just one of the many labels you'll find at Art up. The shop represents young designers from Vienna's art schools, so you can find some unique and exclusive items here. Milch is designed by Cloed Baumgartner. She makes dresses from men's trousers. Transgender, funky styles.

245 EVA BLUT

Kühfussgasse 2
Innere Stadt ①
+43 (0)1 890 65 60 15
evablut.com

Eva Blut's speciality is wearable bags, with different shapes. Her designs are the classics of the future. Her collection is always timeless, light and sleek. All the bags are designed in Vienna and manufactured in Europe, using only the finest quality leathers. Her elegant objects are the future of the Viennese leathergoods tradition.

5
HIGH-QUALITY
shops to explore

---

246 INA KENT

Neubaugasse 34
Neubau ⑤
+43 (0)699 195 410 90
inakent.com

Ina Kent's slogan is 'Bags tell stories'. She started out with just one small shop, but now she has two in the best shopping areas in town. Her beautiful bags are timeless and produced by a small workshop in Karachi. From the selection of the raw hide to the tannery and the production, here every step of the production process is fair and transparent.

247 FURIOS

Dornbacher
Strasse 4
Hernals ⑪
+43 (0)664 221 44 22
fur-ios.com

At Furios upcycling is everything. Bring grandma's fur coat and let them transform it into something completely new. Here wearing fur is not old-fashioned. It's sustainable too: No animals are harmed if you upcycle an old fur and it is more environmentally-friendly than polyester.

248 WALL

Westbahnstrasse 5-A
Neubau ⑤
+43 (0)1 524 47 28
kaufhauswall.com

Everything here is of outstanding quality, including the clothes, the accessories, the books and the care products by brands such as Barbara I Gongini, First aid to be injured, Trippen, Das golden Wiener Herz, Saskia Diez, Scandinaviaform, Sassoon and Shu Uemura.

249 DIE BUNTIQUE

Kirchengasse 26
Neubau ⑤
diebuntique.at

'Von Hand mit Herz', this is the mission of the three women who founded Die Buntique to produce handmade toys for babies and toddlers. They know that the most important thing for you is your child's safety so they think a lot about what they are making. See what they do on facebook or Insta.

250 FEINEDINGE

Margareten-
strasse 35
Margareten ④
+43 (0)1 954 09 18
feinedinge.at

Feinedinge is handmade porcelain. You can see all the tablewares, accessories and lamps they produce in their sleek white showroom. The studio was founded by Sandra Haischberger, who studied with Matteo Thun. Silvie Siegl, Judith Giefing and Lilith Matthews work with her.

The 5 best shops for
MEN'S FASHION

---

251 SONG

Praterstrasse 11
Leopoldstadt ②
+43 (0)1 532 28 58
song.at

Song is kind of an institution in Vienna: The Korean-Viennese owner opened a smaller shop in Vienna's first district with some extraordinary new fashions you couldn't find anywhere else. Today she still is the leading figure for experimental high-class fashion – also for men. Ring the bell, it's worth it.

252 AMICIS MEN

Tuchlauben 14
Innere Stadt ①
+43 (0)1 513 21 10
amicis.at

Amicis is the place to go for designer fashion for men. Not as experimental as Song, but classic and simple designs. Here you can find Alexander McQueen, Balenciaga, Givenchy, Lanvin, Tom Ford, Valentino and many others. For the elegant man who has already found his style.

253 NEON

Mahlerstrasse 7
Innere Stadt ①
+43 (0)1 513 21 32
neon-fashion.com

Neon's slogan is 'slightly different'. They sell Italian chic and masculine sportswear, as well as smart business looks. Try leading international brands like Belstaff, Drykorn or newcomers like Transit, Thom Krom or Hannes Roether.

254 PARK

Mondscheingasse 20
Neubau ⑤
+43 (0)1 526 44 14
park-onlinestore.com

The shop itself is worth seeing: the white purist architecture gives fashion enough space to work its magic on two floors. Start by window shopping outside. Inside you find a selection of items by Petar Petrov, Raf Simons, Acne Studios and many more.

255 SLOWEAR

Weihburggasse 9
Innere Stadt ①
slowear.com

Slowear produces garments for connoisseurs. Their ethical fashion caters to men with a personality and culture. Slowear comes from Italy. All the accessories and footwear of Officina Slowear are still exclusively made in Italy. You also find brands like Incotex, Zanone and Glanshirt here.

251 SONG

5 of the best shops for
WOMEN'S FASHION

256 SCHELLA KANN

Spiegelgasse 15
Innere Stadt ①
+43 (0)1 997 27 55
schellakann.com

Schella Kann is Vienna's iconic fashion label. Its creative director Anita Aigner designs two ready-to-wear collections a year. She is famous for her pure, often mono-coloured style. But since autumn/winter 2018 she has moved on to colourful check-prints. Get inspired.

257 MICHEL MAYER

Singerstrasse 7
Innere Stadt ①
+43 (0)1 967 40 55
michelmayer.at

The designs of Michaela Mayer (No mistake, the brand's name is indeed Michel Mayer) are multifunctional and moving. You have to try on her dresses to understand their *rafinesse*. You can often find videos of her work on her homepage. Check out her semi-couture collection. You can find it in New York, L.A. and Vienna.

258 SUSANNE BISOVSKY

Seidengasse 13
Neubau ⑤
+43 (0)699 111 767 55
bisovsky.com

The story of her life reads like a fairy tale. She came from the tiny village of Gumpoldskirchen near Vienna, launching an international career, starting with her training with Vivienne Westwood and Helmut Lang. Her trademark is latex. Her *Shiftkleid* was shown at MoMA in New York in 2017.

259 LENA HOSCHEK

Goldschmied-
gasse 7-A
Innere Stadt ①
+43 (0)1 503 092 00
lenahoschek.com

Traditional costumes interpreted in a new way. Lena Hoschek started to do this early on – years before it was a hype like today. All her collections are exemplary of her distinctive style, with colourful dresses, knitwear, tops and accessories. The best place to buy a Hoschek *Dirndl* or a petticoat. Katy Perry already did.

260 UTE PLOIER

Ruedigergasse 8/3
Margareten ④
+43 (0)1 943 12 56
uteploier.com

Ute Ploier launched a menswear brand in 2003 – and you can still feel this in her womenswear line till today. In a very positive sense. She believes in a sensual yet edgy femininity. Here the attitude is easy to wear but sophisticated. With a love for details, like in her menswear line.

259 LENA HOSCHEK

5 great places to buy
GLASSES

261 BRILLEN-MANUFAKTUR

Neubaugasse 18
Neubau ⑤
+43 (0)1 523 82 00
brillenmanufaktur.at

As the name *Manufaktur* indicates, here *manus* (Latin for hand) is all that counts. The team of the Brillenmanufaktur really put lots of effort into finding the right specs for you. It is not just about design. They are all experts and trained opticians. A place that is both stylish and useful: see the world through new glasses.

262 VIU EYEWEAR × WE BANDITS

Neubaugasse 36
Neubau ⑤
+43 (0)720 815 441
de.shopviu.com

There was no such thing as a fashion and eyewear shop in Vienna. VIU sells Swiss design that is handmade in Italy and Japan. Very fancy, quite expensive. If you don't have the time to come to the shop then take them up on their Try-at-home offer and get up to four models sent to your home.

263 DIE BRILLE PHILIPP

Josefstädter-strasse 70
Josefstadt ⑥
+43 (0)1 406 22 33
diebrille-philipp.at

Philipp Bischel sells new and vintage models. But best of all: he provides excellent support when it comes to choosing the right glasses for you. Bischel is not a star optician. All he wants to do is help you find what you need.

264 SCHAU-SCHAU

Rotenturmstrasse 11
Innere Stadt ①
+43 (0)1 533 45 84
schau-schau.at

Schau-Schau is a classic. The optician Peter Kozich is an expert. All glasses are handmade. Choose between acetate (made of cotton), horn or metal. You can even find models in 18 carat gold (designed by Christa Karas-Waldheim). Ask for the vintage collection from the eighties. It's cult.

265 ACE & TATE

Neubaugasse 40
Neubau ⑤
+43 (0)720 882 947
aceandtate.de

'Me, myself and I' is the slogan of Ace & Tate. Young and fresh. See their unisex sunglasses that were created in collaboration with the menswear label CMMN SWDN consisting of three acetate and three metal frames. Dive into youth subculture.

262 VIU EYEWEAR × WE BANDITS

5
ORGANIC ONLY
spots

---

266 **GUTER STOFF**

Glockengasse 9
Leopoldstadt ②
+43 (0)699 133 843 57
guterstoff.com

Guter Stoff is a play on words: Stoff means stuff and woven fabric. And here they sell environmentally-friendly fair trade stuff only, including T-shirts for men and women, hoodies, anysex accessories, gym bags... all organic, fair trade, or recycled. Ask for a print of your own logo.

266 GUTER STOFF

267 MARONSKI

Neubaugasse 7
Neubau ⑤
+43 (0)699 113 474 54
maronski.at

Maronski got its name from the so-called Maroons, a Caribbean indigenous group with a woman as their leader. Since 2006, the designer Martina Meixner has developed her own brand. All organic and produced in Europe. At my.maronski you can design your individual dress using her modular system.

268 SAINT CHARLES APOTHEKE

Gumpendorfer-
strasse 30
Mariahilf ⑤
+43 (0)1 586 13 63
saint-charles.eu

Alexander Ehrmann, the founder of Saint Charles Apotheke, brings the long tradition of his family business into modern times. He sells natural cosmetics, based on a holistic view of human beings, combining traditional knowledge with modern concepts. All organic.

269 MODE AUS DER NATUR

Barnabitengasse 3
Mariahilf ⑤
+43 (0)1 581 32 00
modeausdernatur.at

The owner and designer Ingrid Frank started her business in 1994. Initially she only sold baby and childrenswear. In 2001, she started designing womenswear. In 2007 she changed the name of her shop from 'Popolina Galeria' to 'Mode aus der Natur', so you can see at a glance what she's selling.

270 ANZÜGLICH

Theobaldgasse 9/1b
Mariahilf ⑤
+43 (0)1 909 36 13
anzueglich.at

Organic and fair trade. The designer Bawi Koszednar is known for her individual style and a special type of femininity that is self-confident and strong. Many of the pieces can be wrapped around the body, in your own, individual way. Since 2009, the collection is manufactured in Cusco/Peru in a workshop where mainly deaf women work.

5 places loved by
DESIGNERS

---

271 PAPIERHAFEN

Franz-Josefs-Kai 27
Innere Stadt ⓘ
+43 (0)1 533 19 28
papierhafen.at

Papierhafen means paper harbour – and that is exactly what it is. A harbour of old-fashioned goods. If you love the smell of good old paper, then this is the place for you. The owner Heidrun Seelke sells all kinds of papers and a selection of pencils, inks and fountain pens. Everything a lover of hand writing needs.

272 POLIFORM

Franz-Josefs Kai 47
Innere Stadt ⓘ
+43 (0)1 533 56 00
spaetauf.at

The showroom is a meeting place for architects and designers. It is the headquarters of the Italian company Varenna, a well-known producer of up-to-date kitchen design. If you already have a perfect kitchen: don't worry. Combine it with some furniture by Desalto and Riva 1920. Get inspired!

273 EOOS

Zelinkagasse 2/6
Innere Stadt ⓘ
+43 (0)1 405 39 87
eoos.com

They are famous for their furniture designs. And they are quite philosophical, taking a keen interest in poetic things like rituals, plants, ancient high tech, simultaneity and transformation. Martin Bergmann, Gernot Bohmann and Harald Gründl are Eoos. They love a paradox.

274 SAFRAN + CIE

Werdertorgasse 12
Innere Stadt ①
+43 (0)1 532 09 94
safrancie.com

There was a time when carpets were out of fashion. But this has since changed! You don't have to travel to the orient for very fine carpets and kelims. Safran + Cie produces traditional handmade home textiles and carpets. Here you can also find modern interpretations of an old motif.

275 INDIE

Strobelgasse 2
Innere Stadt ①
+43 (0)1 512 51 96
india.co.at

Indie still is one of the most beautiful shops in the city. The timeless beautiful design of the shop alone is worth seeing. The main colour is black, so the whole spectrum of all the colourful textiles you find here glitters like a rainbow. Silk and other woven fabrics as well as beachwear and pyjamas.

274 SAFRAN + CIE

WU-CAMPUS

25 BUILDINGS TO ADMIRE

The 5 most spectacular
SKYSCRAPERS

—————

276 POSTHOCHHAUS
    Herrengasse 6-8
    Innere Stadt ①

This was Vienna's first skycraper and it caused quite a commotion when it was built in 1931 by the architects Theiß & Jaksch. It is 52 metres high and has 235 apartments. The architects used a trick. When you stand in Herrengasse and look up, you can't see how high it is because of the stepped design. Very smart of them.

277 DC TOWER
    Donau City-Strasse 7
    Donaustadt ⑦
    +43 (0)1 225 120
    viennadc.at

The DC Tower is the highest building in Austria. DC stands for Donau City, an area near VIC (Vienna International Centre) where many office buildings were built in recent years. The architect Dominique Perrault created a cool black landmark. Have dinner in the restaurant on the top floor.

278 DELUGAN MEISSL TOWER

Wienerberg City
Wienerberg ⑧

Wienerberg used to be a working-class district for very poor people, who produced the bricks for building the Emporers Ringstrasse and its famous buildings. The so called *Ziegelböhm* (bricklayers from Bohemia) were mainly from the eastern parts of the former empire. Today this fancy district overlooks the city, the Delugan Meissl Tower – named after the architects – being one of its landmarks.

279 DONAUTURM

AT: DONAUPARK
Donauturmstrasse 8
Donaustadt ⑦
+43 (0)1 263 35 72
donauturm.at

It stood out when it was built (from 1962–1964) and it still does. Donauturm is 252 metres high and has a breathtaking restaurant 170 metres above the ground, which rotates very slowly, so you have a beautiful view of different parts of Vienna. Some people get seasick.

280 VIENNA INTERNATIONAL CENTRE

Wagramer Strasse 5
Donaustadt ⑦
+43 (0)1 260 60
unov.org/unov/ en/vic.html

A fabulous example of seventies architecture. The impressive Vienna International Centre (VIC) has been home to numerous international organisations since 1979. Visitors can learn about the work of the United Nations and experience the striking architecture and vibrant, cosmopolitan atmosphere of the VIC during the daily tours.

5 interesting
COMMUNITY
BUILDINGS

---

281 KARL MARX HOF
**Heiligenstädter
Strasse 82
Döbling** ⑲

Karl Marx Hof is probably the most famous of all Viennese municipal tenement buildings. This massive building is over 1000 metres long, making it the longest residential building in the world. Only 20% of it is covered. The rest of it consist of community yards and gardens.

282 GOETHEHOF
**Schüttaustrasse 1
Donaustadt** ⑦

During the civil war in 1935, the socialists used this building as a stronghold. The building was even attacked by the air force during the heavy fighting that ensued. Large parts of the building were destroyed but have since been rebuilt and turned into modern apartments.

283 RABENHOF
**Rabengasse 3
Landstrasse** ③
dasrotewien.at

In the early thirties, Vienna was ruled by the socialist party. As part of their policy, they built some huge community housing projects. Rabenhof is one of the municipal tenement buildings that were built under their supervision. In addition to the many apartments, Rabenhof also had a cinema, which has since been transformed into a theatre.

284 LASALLE-HOF

Lasallestrasse 40
Leopoldstadt ②

Lasalle-Hof is also a relic of the thirties, when the city was called red Vienna. It's a good example of a municipal housing project of this era. Typically, it doesn't just have apartments, but also kindergartens, pools, and laundry facilities.

285 REUMANNHOF

Margareten-
gürtel 100-110
Margareten ④

Reumannhof is unusually representative for a municipal housing project. Have a look at its main courtyard and you will discover water fountains. Originally the design featured 16 floors but only eight where built. It's quite impressive anyway.

281 KARL MARX HOF

5
SWIMMING POOLS
worth seeing

---

286 AMALIENBAD

Reumannplatz 23
Favoriten ⑨
+43 (0)1 607 47 47
wien.gv.at

Amalienbad was one of the most modern and beautiful indoor pools in Europe when it was built in the twenties. At the time, this area was a poor working-class district. The pool was a gift from the city's government to the people and was appreciated by rich people too.

286 AMALIENBAD

287 GÄNSEHÄUFEL

Moissigasse 21
Donaustadt ⑦
+43 (0)1 269 90 16
gaensehaeufel.at

Gänsehäufel is an island right in the middle of the city. The body of water surrounding it was originally part of the Donau, but was cut off from the main river since it was straightened. The baths were rebuilt in 1948 by the architects Max Fellerer and Eugen Wörle. Part of it is still a nudist area.

288 BUNDESBAD ALTE DONAU

Arbeiterstrandbad-
strasse 93
Donaustadt ⑦
+43 (0)1 263 36 67
burghaupt
mannschaft.at

This swimming pool is ideal for families, because it has a children's area. It's easy to get here, especially with public transport. Just take the U1 to Alte Donau. Enjoy the interesting architecture, which dates from 1919.

289 STADTHALLENBAD WIEN

Hütteldorfer-
strasse 2-H
Rudolfsheim-
Fünfhaus ⑪
+43 (0)1 890 176 48 90
wienersportstaetten.at

This indoor pool (by the famous architect Roland Rainer) is still a huge, modern pool, after its complex renovation, and especially interesting for professional swimmers. Swimming associations train there and schoolchildren learn to swim here. They also organise swimming and high diving competitions here.

290 SCHÖNBRUNNER-BAD

Schlosspark
Schönbrunn
Hietzing ⑧
+43 (0)1 817 53 53
schoenbrunnerbad.at

This cute little pool is located in the park of the famous Schönbrunn palace. It was used as a training area for British soldiers in the past. Nowadays it is mainly popular with families. The pool is surrounded by beautiful old trees. See the contrast between old and new.

5 *impressive examples of*
JUGENDSTIL

---

291 SECESSION

Friedrichstrasse 12
Innere Stadt ① ④
+43 (0)1 587 53 07
secession.at

The Secession was founded by a group of artists-including Gustav Klimt – who wanted to break with traditional art movements. It was meant to be an alternative place for exhibitions and still is. They organised a crowdfunding for the renovation of the 1400 golden leaves of the huge golden sphere on top of its roof.

292 OBERES BELVEDERE

Prinz-Eugen-
Strasse 27
Landstrasse ③
+43 (0)1 795 570
belvedere.at

Oberes Belvedere is one of two palaces the famous Prince Eugen built for himself. It's a beautiful, representative building and home to a famous art gallery. The Austrian State Treaty was signed by Leopold Figl in 1955 in its marble hall. Take a walk around the baroque park to see the fountains.

293 KIRCHE AM STEINHOF

Baumgartner Höhe 1
Penzing ⑪
+43 (0)1 910 601 10 07

Located on top of a hill, this church overlooks Vienna. The building itself is an important piece of Jugendstil architecture by Otto Wagner. While it is the church of a psychiatric hospital nowadays, you can still visit it.

294 ÖSTERREICHISCHE POSTSPARKASSE

Georg Coch-Platz 2
Innere Stadt ①
+43 (0)1 534 533 30 88
ottowagner.com

Although it was designed by Otto Wagner, this building is rather extraordinary. A great place to see some impressive architecture. Otto Wagner's motto was: "What is impractical can never be beautiful." You can still feel this when you are inside this extraordinary building that originally was a post office.

295 OTTO WAGNER HOFPAVILLION

Schönbrunner
Schlossstrasse
Hietzing ⑧
+43 (0)1 877 15 71
wienmuseum.at

This building was originally meant to be an underground train station and was built especially for the emperor and his entourage. He didn't use it very often. To be accurate, he only used it twice in his life. But it's an interesting building anyway.

294 ÖSTERREICHISCHE POSTSPARKASSE

5 examples of
MODERN
ARCHITECTURE

___

296 GASOMETER

Döblerhofstrasse
Erdberg ⑨
wiener-gasometer.at

These four huge, cylindrical buildings originally were gas tanks. In 2001, they were transformed into a shopping centre, a concert hall, offices and also apartments. Nowadays they are an interesting mix of old and new. Guided tours available.

297 ZAHA-HADID-HAUS

Spittelauer Lände 10
Alsergrund ⑥

Zaha Hadid was also asked to design a residential complex right next to the Donaukanal – and she did. Unfortunately the building is also right next to Spittelauer Lände, a lively street, which is why nobody wanted to live there until it was converted into student housing. Good architecture.

298 WOTRUBA KIRCHE

Rysergasse/
Georgsgasse
Liesing ⑧
+43 (0)1 888 904 56
georgenberg.at

The 'Church of the Most Holy Trinity' is its official name, but it's called Wotruba Kirche after its creator Fritz Wotruba, one of Austria's most famous sculptors. The church building is so experimental that there were some protests when it was built.

299 T-CENTER
Rennweg 97-99
Landstrasse ③

It looks like a huge boat is sailing through the *St. Marx* district but this is actually an office building. An impressive one too, that is adored by critics. It was designed by the architects Günther Domenig, Herfried Peyker and Hermann Eisenköck.

300 WU-CAMPUS
Welthandelsplatz 1
Leopoldstadt ②
+43 (0)1 313 360
wu.ac.at

The whole campus of the Wirtschaftsuniversität Wien (university of economics) opened in 2013 and was designed by various important architects: Sir Peter Cook and his Crab Studio/London designed the D3/AD departments while the administration, the library and the learning centre were created by Zaha Hadid Architects. Hitoshi Abe developed the student centre. It's open to the public, so just walk in and look around.

300 WU-CAMPUS

ZENTRALFRIEDHOF WIEN

50 PLACES TO DISCOVER IN VIENNA

5
FILMS SHOT IN VIENNA

301 MAYERLING

Mayerling 3
Mayerling
+43 2258 2275
karmel-mayerling.org

Mayerling is a romantic tragedy from 1968, which tells the true story of Crown Prince Rudolf of Austria and his mistress Baroness Mary Vetsera. Mayerling was the imperial family's hunting lodge, where the lovers were found dead. See Omar Sharif as Rudolf and Catherine Deneuve as Mary and then visit the place. Nowadays it is home to a convent of the Carmelite Sisters, but they do have a visitor centre.

302 BEFORE SUNRISE

AT: FRIEDHOF DER
NAMENLOSEN
Albener Hafen
Simmering ⑨
friedhof-der-namenlosen.at

The Cemetery of the Nameless is one of the places where Richard Linklater had his protagonists Ethan Hawke and Julie Delpy spend a night in Vienna in his film *Before Sunrise*. From 1840 until 1900, 478 unknown dead people were buried here in the forest near Albener Hafen, a harbour situated along the Donau. Possibly the scariest scene in this romantic drama.

303 DER DRITTE MANN
**Various places
all over town**

The Third Man is a famous film noir directed by Carol Reed and the most famous film to be set in post-war Vienna, in the year 1949 when the city was still divided in four sectors. Follow its stars Orson Welles, Joseph Cotten and Trevor Howard as they navigate Vienna's sewers or on the Giant Ferris Wheel.

304 SISSI
**AT: MICHAELER KIRCHE
Michaelerplatz 4-5
Innere Stadt ⓘ
+43 (0)1 533 80 00
Erzdioezese-wien.at**

To some, *Sissi* is the epitome of Austrian film. The film, which is set in Vienna and dates from 1955, was directed by Ernst Marischka and is the first in a trilogy about Empress Elisabeth of Austria, who was also called Sissi. Romy Schneider plays the part of the empress. We see her at Schönbrunn Palace and St. Michaels Church, where her wedding took place.

305 THE LIVING DAYLIGHTS
James Bond

The first of two films with Timothy Dalton and the fifteenth in the James Bond series. In 1987, they filmed several outdoor shots around Volksoper, with inside shots of a concert hall in Vienna's Sofiensäle. Fun fact: the story itself takes place in Bratislava, the capital of Slovakia, which was still a part of communist Czechoslovakia at the time. The city is just 80 kilometres from Vienna.

5 nice
FREE BATHING
places

306 COPA CAGRANA
AT: COPA BEACH
Donauinsel ⑦
wien-konkret.at

Copa Cagrana is a fun twist on the name of Brasil's famous Copa Cabana. There's no sea here, but you can bathe in the beautiful Neue Donau. When the Donau was straightened between 1972 and 1988, they built an artificial island here. These days, you can swim here and practise all kinds of outdoor sports. Easy to get to with U1.

VIEW ON DONAUINSEL AND DONAUKANAL

307 MOSQUITO
Raffineriestrasse 8
Donaustadt ⑦

Walk southwards from Copa Cagrana to a wilder part of the Donauinsel and enter the Donau-Auen National Park. Head to the Mosquito bar for toilets and a bite to eat. The only downside: the many mosquitos in summertime.

308 STROMBUCHT
Dampfschiff-
haufen 10
Alte Donau ⑦
wien.gv.at/liegewiese

Alte Donau, or the old Donau, is also a former branch of the Donau and has excellent water quality. The water here is stagnant so it is safe to swim with children. At Dampfschiffhaufen there are plenty of allotments as the Viennese like to head out on the weekend. A very laidback atmosphere.

309 WAKEBOARD LIFT
Am Wehr 1
Donauinsel ⑦
wakeboardlift.at

There is only one wakeboard lift in Vienna: the one at Donauinsel is the preferred meeting point for a young and sporty crowd. Come and watch them, even if you're not the sporty type. Have a bite to eat at wake_up, the nice restaurant with a waterfront terrace. Easy to get to with U2.

310 DECHANTLACKE
Dechantweg
Donaustadt ⑦
donauauen.at

The Donau-Auen National Park has a long-standing tradition of skinny-dipping. If swimming naked is not your cup of tea, then stay away. Check at the Nationalparkhaus where bathing is allowed in the National Park. Explore this wonderful slice of nature on foot or by bike.

5 great places for
SKATING & SPORTS

---

311 SKATE PARK PRATER

Rustenschacher-allee 1
Leopoldstadt ②

Prater used to be the royal family's hunting grounds. In 1766, it opened to the public and nowadays it is an important green area for all kinds of leisure activities. It is divided in the Wurstelprater (amusement park) and the green Prater. It also has the coolest skate park. All levels!

312 DONAUPARK

Donaupark
Donaustadt ⑦

The Donaupark opened together with the Donauturm for the international garden show in 1964. Measuring 604.000 square metres, it is actually quite large. It has retained its sixties look and feel and architecture though. As it is near the UNO-City you'll find a very international crowd here. A good place for a run or a bungee jump.

313 SKATEPLAZA

Neubaugürtel 30
Neubau ⑤

Vienna is a very green city. More than half of the city is made up of green space. But not every district is as green. There are plenty of places to exercise in the more urban areas however. Check out Skateplaza in Neubau: small, but beautiful.

314 DONAUINSEL
Kletterpark
Kaisermühlen-
damm 53
Donauinsel ⑦
+43 (0)660 532 62 62
donauinsel-
kletterpark.at

There are various climbing halls in Vienna but this spot is the best in summer. It is situated on the Donauinsel and you can easily get there by public transport (U1 and a short walk). You can combine climbing with other activities like swimming or roller blading. Plan a day trip.

315 WALDSEILPARK
AT: KAHLENBERG
Josefsdorf 47
Grinzing ⑩
+43 (0)1 320 04 76
waldseilpark-
kahlenberg.at

This climbing park is located in the woods on Kahlenberg. There are 18 courses, with three levels of difficulty. Work on your balance while you enjoy the beautiful view. You can see the entire city from here. Try the zip lines and explore Vienna's green lung, the Wienerwald. Children welcome.

311 SKATE PARK PRATER

5 very special
FOUNTAINS

316 WASSERSPIELPLATZ DONAUINSEL
Donauinsel ⑦
+43 (0)1 400 080 42

This 5000-square-metre-large water playground is a highlight for children – and the child in you. Explore its rivers, waterfalls and lakes. Open from May till September. There is an area where you can relax in deck chairs. No dogs, no smoking.

317 GLORIETTE
Schönbrunner Schlossstrasse 47
Hietzing ⑧
schoenbrunn.at

The Gloriette was built in 1775, is situated at the highest point of the Schönbrunn gardens and at one time was the dining room of Emperor Franz Josef I. From here you can see the castle and several fountains. Nowadays there is an elegant cafe here.

318 HOCHSTRAHL-BRUNNEN
Schwarzenberg-platz
Landstrasse ③

Come and visit Hochstrahlbrunnen in the dark when it is lit in several colours: red, pink, yellow, blue and green. A real *fontaine lumineuse* as the French say. It was built in 1873 when the so-called Wiener Hochquellwasserleitung was finished. Today it still transports crystal clear drinking water from the mountains to the city.

319 **DONNERBRUNNEN**

Neuer Markt
Innere Stadt ①

The fountain's real name is
Providentialbrunnen – but nobody could
pronounce it when it was built in 1739.
Donner was the artist's name. It was a
meeting point for various subcultures
in the eighties, like the mods. Fun fact:
under Maria Theresia the nudity of the
sculptures was considered scandalous.

320 **MUSEUMS-QUARTIER BRUNNEN**

MuseumsQuartier ⑤
mqw.at

The fountain in MuseumsQuartier is the
new place to meet and hang out. It is
situated in front of Kunsthalle, between
Leopold Museum and mumok. If you are
tired from all your wandering and seeing
all that art, just take a break and cool
your sore feet in the fountain. It is strictly
forbidden – but no one cares.

5
BOOKS SET IN VIENNA

321 RETURN TO VIENNA
By Hilde Spiel

Hilde Spiel was an excellent journalist and writer, born in Vienna 1911. Her career was interrupted by the Nazis, when she was forced to flee as a political activist and because she was Jewish. She returned to Vienna as a British journalist in 1946. Read her articles in the book *Return to Vienna* and learn more about Austria's history.

323 HELDENPLATZ

322 BORN-WHERE
By Robert Schindel

Robert Schindel is a famous Austrian author, essayist and lyricist. *Born-Where* (original version *Gebürtig*, which means native) was his debut novel. His story, which starts in eighties Vienna, is a reflection on offenders and victims. It discusses World War II, the Nazis, the Jews, and the future generations.

323 HELDENPLATZ
By Thomas Bernhard
Innere Stadt ①

Visit Heldenplatz, find a place to sit under the old trees on the edge of the meadow and start reading. *Heldenplatz* (origal version *Heldenplatz*) is a 1988 drama by the Austrian author and playwright Thomas Bernhard. He is famous for his cutting analysis of society – and his black humour. After you have read this book, you'll see the place in a different light.

324 BURGTHEATER
By Elfriede Jelinek
Innere Stadt ①

The Nobel Prize winner Elfriede Jelinek wrote a play about Burgtheater, Austria's most famous theatre. It tells the story of three famous actors, Paula Wessely, her husband Attila Hörbiger and his brother Paul, and is a statement on the political situation in Austria, past and present.

325 WIE DIE TIERE
By Wolf Haas
Leopoldstadt ②

And now something completely different: Wolf Haas is a real comedian. His crime novels are often situated in Vienna. In *Wie die Tiere* he tells a fascinating story about animal lovers and misanthropes. This time the killer is wandering around beautiful Augarten Park. Follow in his footsteps.

5 cosy
CO-WORKING SPACES
in Vienna

---

326 ZIMMER NUMMER ACHT

Zimmermanngasse 8
Alsergrund ⑥
+43 (0)678 121 64 95
zi8.at

Maybe you want to stay a little longer, in which case you might need a co-working space. It is also an easy way to get to know people. Zi8 is a nice and cosy co-working cafe with desks for rent. It costs just 15 euro per day. You can also rent the whole place for an event.

327 COCOQUADRAT

Wiedner Hauptstrasse 65
Wieden ④
+43 (0)1 503 06 06
cocoquadrat.com

The more often you use it the cheaper it gets. The first 10 hours will set you back 3 euro an hour, but once you've reached 40 hours, an hour will cost you 2 euro. Better yet: the first 10 hours are free. Fully-equipped kitchen. You also can rent a meeting room. Located near Naschmarkt, so there are plenty of bars and restaurants nearby.

328 IMPACT HUB

Lindengasse 56
Neubau ⑤
+43 (0)1 522 71 43
vienna.impacthub.net

Impact Hub is one of the biggest co-working spaces in Vienna. Here they have different options: a desk for a few days a week, meeting rooms or a full membership including different events. Enjoy the Berlin style of the open, light loft. Very international, English as a main language.

329 COSPACE

Gumpendorfer-
strasse 65
Mariahilf ⑤
+43 (0)1 535 50 05
co-space.net

CoSpace offers an all-inclusive solution: space, communication, meeting facilities. As a member you enjoy a growing list of discounts and special offers from partner institutions. Centrally-located in fancy Gumpe as Gumpendorferstrasse is also called.

330 LOFFICE

Schottenfeldgasse 85
Neubau ⑤
+43 (0)699 150 996 85
lofficeworking.com

Kata and Panni Klementz are the founders of Loffice. This loft and events venue for up to 100 people is also a co-working and art space. A great place to tap into Vienna's start-up scene. You don't necessarily need to go there to work.

5 houses
WHERE FAMOUS MUSICIANS LIVED

331 **JOHANN STRAUSS HAUS**

Praterstrasse 54
Leopoldstadt ②
+43 (0)1 214 01 21
wienmuseum.at

Walk along beautiful Praterstrasse Boulevard and discover the Johann Strauss Haus. Here Johann Strauss (son) composed his famous Waltz *An der schönen blauen Donau*, which some consider to be Austria's unofficial anthem, in 1867. See some of his instruments, photos and learn more about how he lived.

332 **STRAUSS MUSEUM**

Müllnergasse 3
Alsergrund ⑥
+43 (0)1 310 31 06
strauss-museum.at

The Strauss Museum focusses on the whole Strauss family: Johann Strauss (father), Johann Strauss (son), Josef and Eduard Strauss. Here you can learn all about these famous composers in 15 chapters, about their life and work.

333 **MOZART HAUS VIENNA**

Domgasse 5
Innere Stadt ①
+43 (0)1 512 17 91
mozarthausvienna.at

Mozart lived and worked in various places. But nowadays there is only one apartment where you can really see how he lived. It was the biggest and most expensive home he could ever afford. He lived here from 1784 to 1787 and composed *Le Nozze di Figaro* and three of his *Haydn-Quartets* here.

334 BEETHOVEN PASQUALATIHAUS

Mölker Bastei 8
Innere Stadt ①
+43 (0)1 535 89 05
wienmuseum.at

The building itself is interesting as it is located on the former city wall. Pasqualatihaus was built in 1797 for Empress Maria Theresia's physician, Johann Baptist Freiherr von Pasqualiti und Osterburg. Beethoven lived here from 1804 until 1815. Today the memorial is part of the Wienmuseum.

335 BEETHOVEN MUSEUM

Probusgasse 6
Döbling ⑩
+43 (0)664 889 508 01
wienmuseum.at

Beethoven lived in Vienna for 35 years, so there are various places where he stayed. Here you can find his former flat and a large Beethoven Museum, which tells the story of his life and where you can hear some of his compositions. The historic house with its old *Pawlatschen* (wooden arcades) gives you a good idea of how people lived at the time.

335 BEETHOVEN MUSEUM

5
VERY UGLY PLACES

---

336 MÜLL-VERBRENNUNGS-ANLAGE SPITTELAU
Spittelauer Lände 45
Alsergrund ⑥

Friedensreich Hundertwasser is a famous Austrian artist who is known for his colourful paintings and objects. He didn't like straight lines, and there are none in his Hunderwasser Kunsthaus in Vienna. In 1987 he decorated the waste incineration plant with his art. Bizarre!

337 ALTE WU
Althanstrasse
Alsergrund ⑥
univie.ac.at

It's as if a UFO landed here. The building of the former university of economics dates from the eighties. When students moved in in 1982 the university was already too small. Nowadays it is located on a brand-new WU-campus. The city is currently thinking about what to do with the building.

338 VERKEHRS-MINISTERIUM

Radetzkystrasse 2
Landstrasse ③
bmvit.at

This resembles a postmodern castle, with its many different colours and towers that form an octagon. When the architect Peter Czernin started building it in 1981, the building was considered state of the art. But nowadays eighties architecture has very few fans. Who knows, maybe the eighties will experience a revival, like in fashion.

339 HAUS DES MEERES

Fritz-Grünbaum
Platz 1
Mariahilf ⑤
+43 (0)1 587 14 17
haus-des-meeres.at

These anti-aircraft blockhouse towers were built by the Nazis during World War II. They are so solid that they were impossible to destroy. Some of them are empty today (like the one in Augarten), but some were given a new use like the Haus des Meeres, which has an aquarium.

340 FRANZ-JOSEFS BAHNHOF

Julius-Tandler-Platz
Alsergrund ⑥

The beautiful train station by Ullmann and Barvicius, which dated from 1872, was demolished (you can see some footage of it in a film called *Mayerling*), and a new building replaced it in 1978. The main idea behind the project was to create a space for offices above the station. Still very ugly.

5 of the best
BIKE TOURS

---

341 FRIEDHOF DER NAMENLOSEN
Starting at Praterstern Leopoldstadt ②
fahrradwien.at

Start at Praterstern in Leopoldstadt and bike through the green Prater till you reach the Donau and Vienna's harbour. You'll not run into traffic on this tour as cars are forbidden in Prater. Enjoy the beautiful Auwald. When you reach Albener Hafen, you are near Friedhof der Namenlosen (see films).

342 HÖHENSTRASSE
Döbling

This trail is not as easy as the first one. As its name indicates, Höhenstrasse leads to the higher parts of Vienna. It will take you through beautiful Wiener Wald but the cobblestones on your way up make this a difficult journey. Enjoy the beautiful view when you have reached your destination.

343 BISAMBERG
Floridsdorf ⑦

You need to be fit to ride up Bisamberg. Take a break in one of the beautiful Heuriger in Stammersdorfer Kellergasse. Or – even better – take a break on your way down so you can have a glass (or two) of wine.

344 SEESTADT ASPERN
Aspern

Seestadt Aspern is a brand-new district in the city. A must-see if you are interested in modern architecture and city planning. Take U2 to get here (a 20-minute journey). You can take your bike on the metro. Then enjoy a relaxed ride in the Seestadt.

345 DONAUINSEL
Donauinsel ⑦

The Donauinsel was built when the Donau was straightened in the seventies. Nowadays there are beautiful beaches, trees and infrastructure here. The artificial island is more than 20 kilometres long and has several bike trails. Check the direction of the often-strong winds before you set off.

344 SEESTADT ASPERN

5
CEMETERIES
worth a visit

---

346 ZENTRALFRIEDHOF WIEN

Simmeringer
Hauptstrasse 234
Simmering ⑨
friedhoefewien.at

'Es lebe der Zentralfriedhof und alle seine Toten!', a song by Austrian singer-songwriter Wolfgang Ambros, is one of the country's unofficial anthems. It reflects the dark side of Austrian identity and black humour. Hear the song and then take a gander around Austria's largest cemetery.

347 SANKT MARXER FRIEDHOF

Leberstrasse 6-8
Landstrasse ③

Today the Sankt Marxer Friedhof is a park and a historical site. It closed in 1874 as a cemetery. The most famous grave you will find here is that of Wolfgang Amadeus Mozart. The famous composer died in 1791 in Vienna and was buried here. The exact location is unknown.

346 ZENTRALFRIEDHOF WIEN

348 HEILIGENSTÄDTER FRIEDHOF

Wildgrubgasse 20
Nussdorf
Döbling ⑩

This cemetery is beautifully situated at the bottom of Nussberg among vineyards. You can easily find it when you walk from Grinzing to Nussdorf. It is one of the oldest in Vienna, dating from 1500. The famous author Ödön von Horváth is buried here.

349 GRINZINGER FRIEDHOF

An den langen
Lüssen 33
Döbling ⑩

This cemetery opened in 1783 and was enlarged and renovated several times in the past 200 or so years. Here can you find several graves of famous people including that of Alma Mahler-Werfel, Alexander von Sacher-Masoch, the famous author Heimito von Doderer and the composer Gustav Mahler.

350 JÜDISCHER FRIEDHOF

Seegasse 9
Alsergrund ⑥
+43 (0)1 4000 8042

The Jüdischer Friedhof Seegasse is the oldest Jewish cemetery in Vienna that was not destroyed. Here you'll find graves from the 16th, 17th and 18th centuries. After World War II, 280 of the 931 graves were rebuilt. Enter through the nursing home in Seegasse.

MUMOK

45 PLACES
FOR CULTURE

5 places for
OFF-THEATRE CULTURE

---

351 **SCHAUSPIELHAUS WIEN**

Porzellangasse 19
Alsergrund ⑥
+43 (0)1 317 01 01
schauspielhaus.at

In 1978, the famous director Hans Gratzer transformed this former cinema into a theatre. In the eighties, George Tabori first performed his experimental work *Der Kreis* here. Today the Schauspielhaus Wien still focusses on experimental theatre.

351 SCHAUSPIELHAUS WIEN

352 TAG WIEN

Gumpendorfer Strasse 67
Mariahilf ⑤
+43 (0)1 586 52 22
dastag.at

A newcomer on the Viennese theatre scene is Tag, which was founded in 2013-2014 by Gernot Plass, who works with an ensemble from all German-speaking countries. They also schedule impro-theatre, workshops and concerts here, so language should not be a problem.

353 WERK X

Oswaldgasse 35-A
Meidling ⑧
+43 (0)1 535 32 00
werk-x.at

A visit to Werk X is always interesting, also from an architectural point of view, as it is located in a former cable-manufacturing plant. The whole area is a good example of successful city planning. Here you see the most exciting and innovative work, always very political. Founded in 2014.

354 KOSMOSTHEATER

Siebensterngasse 42
Neubau ⑤
+43 (0)1 523 12 26
kosmostheater.at

KosmosTheater focusses on gender. Founder Barbara Klein and her team have performed interdisciplinary, political theatre for over 18 years. It is also a meeting place for networking on all kinds of gender-specific questions. Relaunched in autumn 2018, with two new directors, Veronika Steinböck and Gina Salis-Soglio.

355 RABENHOF THEATER

Rabengasse 3
Landstrasse ③
+43 (0)1 712 82 82
rabenhoftheater.com

Rabenhof Theater hosts music performances and readings, cabaret and shows – so not your classical stuff. The theatre is located in twenties building and once was a working-class cinema. In 1990, it became a theatre, always bearing in mind its history as a *Volkstheater*, a community theatre.

5 great
CULTURAL WALKS

---

356 ARCHITECTURE
Otto Wagner Kirche
Hütteldorf ⑪
wienzufuss.at

Vienna is definitely a walking city. Here you don't need a car and you can be a *flaneur*, strolling through the city. Wien zu Fuss provides maps and an app for different walks, including an architectural tour starting from Otto Wagner Kirche.

357 PÖTZLEINSDORFER SCHLOSSPARK
Geymüllergasse 1
Währing ⑪
+43 (0)1 893 00 83
vhs.at

There are many cultural walks but some of them are special. Ask for Franz Linsbauer. He specialises in parks and cemeteries. Choose Pötzleinsdorfer Schlosspark, Wiener Stadtpark, Türkenschanzpark or Die Kapuzinergruft. He knows all about them.

358 ALTSTADT

Albertinaplatz
Innere Stadt ①
wienguide.at

The Verein Wiener Spaziergänge organises several cultural walks. Choose Highlights of the old city, Vienna at first Glance or Jewish Vienna in Leopoldstadt. No reservations required, the tours take place regardless of the weather. Minimum number of participants is three at full price.

359 DRITTE MANN TOUR

Girardipark
Innere Stadt ①④
+43 (0)1 4000 3033
drittemanntour.at

The Third Man is a famous film noir directed by Carol Reed and is the most famous film to take place in post-war Vienna in the year 1949. Follow its stars, Orson Welles, Joseph Cotten and Trevor Howard, as they chase each other down Vienna's sewers. Possibly the greatest British film of all time. Once you heard it you will never forget the music.

360 VIENNA UGLY TOUR

Augarten
Leopoldstadt ②
+43 (0)680 125 43 54
spaceandplace.at/
vienna-ugly

Spaceandplace is working on different projects, all urban, ugly Vienna being just one of them. Everybody knows that Vienna is beautiful. Eugene Quinn and his friends want to take you to the dark side. Follow these rebellious optimists. They want to make some serious points in a humorous way.

5

FESTIVALS
you can't afford to miss

---

361 WIENER FESTWOCHEN

Different venues
+43 (0)1 589 220
festwochen.at

The Wiener Festwochen started out in the fifties and today is the most important multidisciplinary art festival in town combining music theatre, theatre, fine arts, performance, dance, music, installation art and more and more debate and participation in recent years. Be part of it. Always in May and June.

362 JAZZFEST.WIEN

Wiener Staatsoper and other venues Innere Stadt ①
+43 (0)1 712 42 24
jazzfest.wien

All about jazz and what a variety there is to take in. This summer festival, which is organised in June/July, covers so many different types of music including classical jazz, Afro-Cuban stars, big bands, singer-songwriters. There's bound to be a concert that you'll never forget.

363 IMPULSTANZ

Different venues
+43 (0)1 523 55 58
impulstanz.com

You can literally see when ImPulsTanz is in town, when beautiful young and old people from all over the world converge on the city, from mid-July till mid-August, for performances, workshops, socials, research and specials. See Vienna dancing. Free party every night at Burgtheater Vestibül.

364 VIENNALE
Various cinemas
+43 (0)1 526 59 47
viennale.at

Viennale is Vienna's exciting film festival, taking place every autumn. After the sudden death of Hans Hurch, who was the festival's director for several years, Eva Sangiorgi from Italy will help the festival navigate to new times. She has worked and lived in Mexico for the past 15 years. The festival has always had a very international spirit and will continue to do so in the future.

365 WIEN MODERN
Different venues
+43 (0)1 24 200
wienmodern.at

If you love modern, experimental music, then Wien Modern is the festival for you. It is held in October and November every year and the best musicians, including the Wiener Symphoniker, the Wiener Philharmoniker and the ORF Radio-Symphonieorchester, love to take a risk here. Come and hear the best of the best.

361 WIENER FESTWOCHEN

5 interesting
OFF-TOPIC MUSEUMS

---

366 WIENER KRIMINALMUSEUM

Grosse Sperlgasse 24
Leopoldstadt ②
+43 (0)664 300 56 77
kriminalmuseum.at

This museum presents a different, dark chapter in the history of Vienna. In one of the oldest buildings in Leopoldstadt, you can learn more about the most horrific crimes of this city. The Wiener Kriminalmuseum is located in the Seifensiederhaus, which dates from before 1685. A journey from the Middle Ages to post-war times. Chilling!

367 SIGMUND FREUD MUSEUM

Berggasse 19
Alsergrund ⑥
+43 (0)1 319 15 96
freud-museum.at

Berggasse 19 is one of the most famous addresses in Vienna. This is where Sigmund Freud developed his *Psychoanalyse* before he had to flee the Nazis. In 1971, his former office and apartment was transformed into a museum. The exhibition will be redesigned and expanded in 2020.

370 WELTMUSEUM WIEN

368 TECHNISCHES MUSEUM

Mariahilfer Strasse 212
Hietzing ⑧
+43 (0)1 899 98-0
technischesmuseum.at

It's huge, it has a long history, and it is brand-new. The Technisches Museum opened 100 years ago, on 6 May 1918. Even today, it offers a wide range of interesting objects like old trains and machines. The museum's approach is very contemporary, with programmes for adults and children.

369 WITTGENSTEIN HAUS

Parkgasse 18
Landstrasse ③
+43 (0)1 713 31 64
haus-wittgenstein.at

The famous philosopher Ludwig Wittgenstein designed this house. It was finished in 1926 and is still a gem. And thanks to the Bulgarian embassy, which transformed it into a cultural institute, everyone now can visit both the architecture itself and the temporary exhibitions.

370 WELTMUSEUM WIEN

Heldenplatz
Innere Stadt ①
+43 (0)1 534 305 052
weltmuseumwien.at

The reorganised Weltmuseum (the former Museum of Folk Art) is an ethnological museum in beautiful Hofburg. They are very aware of the colonial impact on the collection, so they recently overhauled, taking into consideration the dignity of every item, like Maori Tangihangas.

The 5 best places for
SLAM POETRY &
LITERATURE

---

371 ALTE SCHMIEDE
Schönlaterngasse 9
Innere Stadt ①
+43 (0)1 512 83 29
alte-schmiede.at

The logo of the place is a hammer. The Alte Schmiede in Vienna's oldest part of the old town was a wrought iron workshop as you can tell by the building's structure. They kept all the tools, which is quite impressive to see. They host readings and panel discussions, but also have a very special music program, so no language problems.

372 LITERATURHAUS WIEN
Seidengasse 13
Neubau ⑤
+43 (0)1 526 204 40
literaturhaus.at

The Literaturhaus is one of the most important places for contemporary literature in Austria. It is the headquarters of IG Autoren Autorinnen and they have a very good public library. They also organise conferences, panel discussions and photo exhibitions. The newspaper archive might also be of interest.

373 ÖSTERREICHISCHE GESELLSCHAFT FÜR LITERATUR

Herrengasse 5
Innere Stadt ①
+43 (0)1 533 81 59
www.ogl.at

The OGL in beautiful Palais Wilcek has plenty of history. It was founded in post-war Austria in the sixties and it was here that Ingeborg Bachmann first read her *Böhmen liegt am Meer* in 1965. Hear her reading in the Mediathek and see all the black and white portraits of the famous writers who came here.

374 POETRYSLAM

AT: SCHWARZBERG
Schwarzenberg-platz 10
Landstrasse ③④
poetryslam.at

Slam poetry has hit Austria! The Poetryslam portal lists all the events and open mics in Vienna and the wider region. Schwarzberg is just one place that hosts these vibrant, international activities. Meet the young crowd, be part of it. It's about language, music, politics, fun.

375 OFFENE BURG

Burgtheater Wien
Innere Stadt ①
+43 (0)1 514 444 140
burgtheater.at

The Burgtheater is Austria's most important theatre. They wanted to open the theatre to all people, young and old, speaking any language which is why Offene Burg was established. Here you can choose from different activities or you can be an actor/actress yourself at VorstellBar. Just be open.

5
CONCERT HALLS
you should definitely visit

---

376 **WIENER KONZERTHAUS**
Lothringerstrasse 20
Landstrasse ③
+43 (0)1 242 002
konzerthaus.at

The Wiener Konzerthaus is an allrounder: here you can enjoy classical music, modern, jazz, world and pop music concerts and they also have a children's programme. With around 500 concerts and events every year, there is something for everyone. Or just come and see the impressive music hall in the building that dates from 1913.

377 **MUSIKVEREIN WIEN**
Musikvereinsplatz 1
Innere Stadt ①④
+43 (0)1 505 81 90
musikverein.at

You know this place! Every year, you can see this beautiful concert hall on TV if you watch the New Year's Concert of the Wiener Philharmoniker. In 2018, the concert was broadcast in 95 countries. The building opened in 1870 after Emperor Franz Joseph donated the land to the Gesellschaft der Musikfreunde.

379 **ARENA WIEN**

378 WIENER STADTHALLE

Roland Rainer Platz 1
Rudolfsheim-
Fünfhaus ⑪
+43 (0)1 981 000
stadthalle.com

Conchita Wurst brought back the Eurovision Song Contest to the Wiener Stadthalle. This is the biggest venue of its kind in Austria and one of the three biggest in Europe. It was designed by the famous architect Roland Rainer in the fifties.

379 ARENA WIEN

Baumgasse 80
Landstrasse ③
+43 (0)1 798 85 95
arena.wien

The Arena is not just Austria's biggest indoor and outdoor concert hall for alternative and indie music, it is a cult venue. It was born out of a youth movement that occupied the former St. Marx slaughterhouse in the seventies and is still an important spot for youth culture in Vienna.

380 MARX HALLE

Karl-Farkas-Gasse 19
Landstrasse ③
+43 (0)1 888 55 25
marxhalle.at

Marx Halle is like a tinier, more conventional sister or brother of Arena. It is nearby, was also part of the former slaughterhouse and a historic building. If you love smallish concerts (not an audience of 8000 and more like in Stadthalle) then this is the place for you.

5

HIDDEN GEMS IN ART HISTORY MUSEUMS

381 BRUEGHEL UNDER A MICROSCOPE

KUNSTHISTORISCHES MUSEUM

Maria-Theresien Platz

Innere Stadt ①

+43 (0)1 525 243 300

khm.at

The Kunsthistorisches Museum of course has the most important collection, but they also organise temporary exhibitions. In 2019, various museums will be celebrating the 450th anniversary of the death of Peter Brueghel the Elder, the greatest 16th-century Flemish painter. Come and see the world's first ever monographic exhibition on Brueghel's work.

382 MARIA ANTHONY VAN DYCK

The KHM's collection is so large that you need to narrow it down. You can't see everything in one visit. Part of the museum's new approach is that they provide help, suggesting different ideas for organising your visit. Why not visit all the Virgin Mary paintings, starting with Anthony van Dyck's for example?

383 GANYMED NATURE

Another option is the changing ideas about nature in the history of art. This is the fifth time that the *Ganymed* series is hosted in the KHM: After Boarding, Ganymed goes Europe, Dreaming and Female, this time the emphasis is on nature. Jacqueline Kornmüller is the director of a living theatre, with actors and artists performing in the museum.

384 GANYMED FEMALE

Ganymed Female focussed on gender. But besides the Ganymed performances, the museum often hosts events on the topic of gender, including special tours every year on International Women's Day (8th of March) that highlight the female gaze in art.

385 TINTORETTO WEISSBÄRTIGER MANN
Bordone Saal
Sitzbank

The famous writer Thomas Bernhard's comedy *Alte Meister* made Tintoretto's *Weissbärtiger Mann* even more famous. In the book, the fictional art critic Reger has been visiting the KHM for over 30 years to see the picture. Since then several visitors have searched for the fictional Bordone room. But the Tintoretto really exists. Go find it!

5 of the best places for
CONTEMPORARY ART

---

386 MUMOK

Museumsplatz 1
Neubau ⑤
+43 (0)1 525 000
mumok.at

As one of several art museums it is located in MuseumsQuartier, the former Hofstallungen. Museum moderner Kunst Stiftung Ludwig Wien, or the full name of mumok, exhibits modern art. Ortner & Ortner designed a black monolith, seeing as the wow factor is inside.

387 SAMMLUNG ESSL IN DER ALBERTINA

Albertinaplatz 1
Innere Stadt ①
+43 (0)1 534 835 40
sammlung-essl.at

Karlheinz Essl built a museum for his own modern art collection in Klosterneuburg near Vienna. In February 2017, the art world finally sat up and noticed it when the Albertina took over the collection because of financial problems.

388 LEOPOLD MUSEUM

MuseumsQuartier
Neubau ⑤
+43 (0)1 525 700
leopoldmuseum.org

Ortner & Ortner Baukunst created this light, white museum as a contrast to the black mumok nearby. Its collection starts in the 19th century, focussing on Egon Schiele of course. But they also have some amazing artworks from the 20th century, which date from before World War II. Combine with mumok.

389 KUNSTHALLE WIEN

Museumsplatz 1
MuseumsQuartier ⑤

Treitlstrasse 2
Wieden ④
+43 (0)1 521 890
kunsthallewien.at

In recent years, Kunsthalle Wien has focussed on participation. You'll often see experimental works in this contemporary art museum. They have no collection of their own, so they organise plenty of different exhibitions. Follow the eagle.

390 21ER HAUS

Arsenalstrasse 1
Favoriten ⑨
+43 (0)1 795 57 00
21erhaus.at

The architect Karl Schwanzer designed this building for the World Expo in 1958. The award-winning design still looks just as fresh today. After being adapted in 2007 by Adolf Krischanitz it now is part of the Belvedere. This house for the 21th century is dedicated to contemporary art. The best opening parties in town!

390 21ER HAUS

5 works you should see in
MUMOK

---

mumok
Museumsplatz 1
Neubau ⑤
+43 (0)1 525 000
mumok.at

391 WIENER AKTIONISMUS

Many people considered Vienna in the early sixties to be a conservative, boring place. It was as if everyone refused to reflect on what happened during World War II. A group of young artists rebelled against this with body orientated activism. The so-called 'Uni-Ferkelei' by Günter *Brus, Otto Muehl and Oswald Wiener* kicked off the *Wiener Aktionismus* movement. Learn more here about how it changed society.

392 ARTE POVERA

Arte Povera comes from Italy. *Povera* means poor. This movement originated in the late sixties and early seventies in Genoa and Rome. The artists used everyday normal materials, like broken glass or wood for their artwork. See some of their works in the often-changing exhibitions in mumok.

393 POP ART

Roy Lichtenstein is perhaps the most famous Pop Art name. His work has been popular since the early years of this movement in the 20th century. And most people also are familiar with the colourful, sometimes comic works of Andy Warhol, Robert Indiana, Jasper Johns, Claes Oldenburg and Robert Rauschenberg. See some of the best here.

394 FLUXUS

Fluxus, from the Latin word for flow, is a sixties art movement. It is not so much about the work of art, but about the concept. Some famous artists of the Avantgarde were affiliated with it, including George Maciunas, Joseph Beuys, Yoko Ono and Nam June Paik. Get inspired by the multimedia installations and concepts.

395 NOCTURNE FRANTIŠEK KUPKA

Born in Bohemia, in the former Austrian-Hungarian monarchy, František Kupka received his art education in Prague and Vienna. See his abstract paintings, which often deal with the occult, raising questions about everything you thought you knew about reality. He assembled a circle of painters around him, including Marcel Duchamp. Kupka is perhaps not as famous, but definitely worth discovering.

PRATER MINIGOLF

25 THINGS TO DO WITH CHILDREN

The 5 most
LAIDBACK
places to eat

---

396 DSCHUNGEL CAFÉ

Museumsplatz 1
MuseumsQuartier ⑤
+43 (0)1 522 07 20 20
dschungelwien.at

The Dschungel Café is basically the foyer of the Dschungel Theatre. Does it all sound very stressful and uncomfortable to you? It's anything but! Everybody is friendly and finds it completely normal to have children playing on the floor here. Families love to come here to experience the relaxed atmosphere.

397 CAFÉ EINFAHRT

Haidgasse 3
Leopoldstadt ②
+43 (0)1 942 68 86
einfahrt-wien.at

After shopping on a Saturday morning in Karmeliter Markt there is only one place to go for a coffee and that's the Café Einfahrt. Besides good coffee, they also serve different breakfasts here. Children love this place because of its famous homemade lemonade. They can play inside and in front of the cafe.

398 GASTHAUS SCHÖNE PERLE

Ecke Leopold/
Grosse Pfarrgasse
Leopoldstadt ②
+43 (0)1 890 32 04
schoene-perle.at

This place is very popular with locals and is well-known for its delicious food. It's a bright open space and very child-friendly. But bear in mind that dogs are strictly forbidden so children can play freely here.

399 LUFTBURG

Waldsteingarten-
gasse Prater 128
Leopoldstadt ②
+43 (0)1 729 49 99
kolarik.at

This place is a mix between an adventure park and a restaurant. While parents eat in the shade, children can play on the various bouncy castles and other attractions. What's more, it's located in the green Wiener Prater. You should definitely take a little walk in the park before or after lunch.

400 MQ KANTINE

Museumsplatz 1
MuseumsQuartier ⑤
+43 (0)1 523 82 39
mq-kantine.at

This is one of the best places to eat for a family after a long day of walking through the city. Children can play in the car-free square of MuseumsQuartier or take a nap on one of the couches there while their parents sit down and enjoy some delicious food. You can eat with your fingers here and no one will care.

5 of the best places to
PLAY

---

401 ZOOM KINDERMUSEUM

Museumsplatz 1
MuseumsQuartier ⑤
+43 (0)1 524 79 08
kindermuseum.at

It's fun, it's interactive, it's educational. The Zoom Kindermuseum essentially is a large playground that teaches children a lot about life. A brilliant concept. Changing expeditions on various topics help them to develop new ideas without even knowing, because they are having so much fun.

402 BAUMKREIS

Himmelstrasse 125
Döbling ⑩
+43 (0)1 406 59 38
himmel.at

There are 40 different trees, arranged in a circle, surrounded by vineyards and nature. Sounds beautiful? Well it is! Like star signs, every tree symbolises a number of dates. Take a walk to find your personal life tree.

403 KINDERINFO WIENXTRA

Museumsplatz 1
MuseumsQuartier ⑤
+43 (0)1 400 084 400
wienxtra.at

This place keeps you informed about every child-friendly event and location in the city. Go there, if you are looking for a family-friendly activity. You'll end up leaving with a good plan and some excited kids.

404 LAINZER TIERGARTEN

Hermesstrasse
Lainzer Tor
Hietzing ⑧
+43 (0)1 400 049 200
lainzer-tiergarten.at

Do you want to experience a forest inside a city? Well, there are about 6000 acres of forest in the west of Vienna. This unique area is a wonderful place for a walk with your children. If you are lucky, you might even spot a wild boar.

405 DONAUINSEL KLETTERPARK

Am Kaisermühlen-
damm 53
Donaustadt ⑦
+43 (0)660 532 62 62
donauinsel-
kletterpark.at

An obstacle course ten metres above the ground… But don't worry, you and your child wear a line and are 100 percent safe the entire time. Definitely exciting and bundles of fun. The trail is open till 10 pm on Friday nights.

402 BAUMKREIS

5 places to
ENJOY CULTURE

---

406 THEATER DER JUGEND

Neubaugasse 38
Neubau ⑤
+43 (0)1 521 10
tdj.at

Theater der Jugend is an organisation that specialises in theatre for young adults and children. Fun fact: it has more subscribers than all three of Vienna's largest theatres together and it's easy to see why. The team have been developing successful theatre productions for several decades and they are really good at it.

409 PRATER KASPERL

407 DSCHUNGEL

Museumsplatz 1
MuseumsQuartier ⑤
+43 (0)1 522 072 020
dschungelwien.at

What can you expect from a place called jungle? Diversity? Experimental performance? Exactly that. The programme offers a varied mix of theatre, dance, music and slam poetry. The performances focus on topics such as being a teenager nowadays dealing with the challenges that young people face today.

408 WUK

Währingerstrasse 59
Alsergrund ⑥
+43 (0)1 401 210
wuk.at

This former factory was peacefully taken over by activists in the early eighties. They created a free community space here that still exists. Exhibitions, concerts, workshops and various other events are organised there. WUK is also the home of many different children's groups.

409 PRATER KASPERL

Wiener
Wurstelprater
Leopoldstadt ②
praterkasperl.com

While the stage curtain is still closed a funny little voice behind asks "Is everybody here?" and all the exited children shout "Yeeeeeeess!". That's how every single performance starts and it is also part of the reason why this place enjoys such a cult status in the area.

410 URANIA PUPPENTHEATER

Uraniastrasse 1
Innere Stadt ①
+43 (0)1 714 36 59
kasperlundpezi.at

The main character Kasperl, a colourful puppet, and his best friend Pezi take us with them on their adventures! They are often inspired by well-known fairy tales and always good fun. A great way to spend an unconventional afternoon.

5 great places for
SPORTS

---

411 WIENER EISTRAUM

Rathausplatz 1
Innere Stadt ①
+43 (0)1 409 00 40
wienereistraum.com

About 8000 square metres of ice in front of the impressive city hall. Open from January till March. The Wiener Eistraum is the best place for ice skating in Vienna with colourful lights, music and lots of fun. The highlight: there are several small and bendy ice trails you can skate on.

412 DIANABAD

Lilienbrunngasse 7-9
Leopoldstadt ②
+43 (0)1 219 818 110
dianabad.at

Dianabad is an indoor pool that is open throughout the year. Because of the many attractions, like a wave pool and a huge waterslide, children will definitely have fun there. But parents will also enjoy their time here. Dianabad also has a large sauna area.

413 SEGELSCHULE HOFBAUER

An der oberen
Alten Donau 191
Donaustadt ⑦
+43 (0)1 204 34 35
hofbauer.at

Segelschule Hofbauer is famous for its well-organised sailing summer courses. Children spend one week learning how to tie special knots and handle a boat. If you are not staying in Vienna that long, do think about having dinner on the large terrace.

414 CLUB DANUBE

Arbeiterstrandbad-
strasse 87-C
Donaustadt ⑦
+43 (0)664 325 53 80
sailing-cd.com

A sailing school that is not as old as Hofbauer, but that is a bit more fun than the others. All the people in the school are easy-going and friendly. Take the underground (U1) and escape the stressful city centre.

415 PRATER MINIGOLF

Prater Hauptallee
Leopoldstadt ②
+43 (0)1 729 20 00

Prater Minigolf is located at the beginning of the Prater's main avenue and therefore both easy to reach and surrounded by trees. It has 18 tricky courses. There is a restaurant next door where you could have a break after playing.

5 places children will love to
DISCOVER

---

416 LILIPUTBAHN

Prater 99
Leopoldstadt ②
+43 (0)1 726 82 36
liliputbahn.at

If you have read Jonathan Swift's classic *Lilliput*, you might suspect what a *Liliputbahn* is. A functional train, but super small. Kids love it. Two out of six locomotives are steam-powered. Try to get on a train that is pulled by one of them.

417 WIENER WURSTELPRATER

Prater
Leopoldstadt ②
+43 (0)1 729 20 00
prater.at

An area full of rollercoasters, ghost trains, carousels and all sorts of other fun things as well as the *Wiener Riesenrad*, a famous landmark, and the Prater Turm, the highest swing carousel in Austria. Just walking through Prater will make all your senses come to life.

418 LANDGUT COBENZEL

Am Cobenzel 96-A
Dornbach
+43 (0)1 328 94 04
landgutcobenzel.at

Learn all about farm life. Landgut Cobenzel is an open farm and is a very informative place, especially for families. Guides will show you around, teaching you everything about animals and agriculture. By the way: the view of Vienna is incredible.

419 TIERGARTEN SCHÖNBRUNN

Seckendorff-
Gudent-Weg
Hietzing ⑧
+43 (0)1 877 929 40
zoovienna.at

Tiergarten Schönbrunn is the world's oldest zoo and was named the best zoo of Europe in 2009, 2011, 2013 and 2015. As you can imagine, it is a wonderful place. Especially famous for its giant pandas. The zoo is involved in endangered species survival plans.

420 PALMENHAUS

Schlosspark
Schönbrunn
Hietzing ⑧
+43 (0)1 877 50 87
bundesgaerten.at

Commissioned by Emperor Franz Joseph in 1882, this palm house is still the biggest in Europe. It's divided into three different sections with plants from three different parts of the world. A great place to enjoy stunning plants and beautiful architecture.

416 LILIPUTBAHN

25 PLACES
TO SLEEP

——————

5 of the best
BOUTIQUE
hotels

421 HOLLMANN BELETAGE

Köllnerhofgasse 6
Innere Stadt ①
+43 (0)1 961 19 60
hollmann-beletage.at

A place that makes you feel as if you are staying with friends. A comfy home in an unfamiliar city. Hollmann Beletage is centrally located in the old town of Vienna. *Beletage* traditionally means first floor which was thought to be the best. It still is best. Nice, purist design, small, but beautiful.

422 ALTSTADT VIENNA

Kirchengasse 41
Neubau ⑤
+43 (0)1 522 66 66
altstadt.at

All about art. The owner Otto E. Wiesenthal is a great art collector – and you can feel it in this special house. This is more than a mere boutique hotel. It's an artwork in itself. With works by Warhol, Niki de Saint Phalle, Prachensky, Leibowitz, Attersee and Helnwein. Every room is different.

423 BOUTIQUEHOTEL STADTHALLE

Hackengasse 20
Rudolfsheim-
Fünfhaus ⑩
+43 (0)1 982 42 72
hotelstadthalle.at

Boutiquehotel Stadthalle is a combination of the old and the new. Part of it consists of a passive house, that was completed in 2009. The other part is an old house from the fin de siècle. The two parts are connected by a cosy lobby, a comfortable breakfast room and a lovely garden.

424 PALAIS COBURG RESIDENZ

Coburgbastei 4
Innere Stadt ①
+43 (0)1 518 18 130
palais-coburg.com

Palais Coburg is a palace. You really will feel like a princess or prince in this historic building that was built in 1845. The ten residential suites vary in size from 71 to 91 square metres. Take your pick from a maisonette style with a cathedral or garden view or a suite with a terrace.

425 HOTEL LAMÉE

Rotenturmstrasse 15
Innere Stadt ①
+43 (0)1 532 22 40
hotellamee.com

A harmonious mix of old and new. This thirties building has a very old Hollywood glamour look and feel. The building's large glass doors open out onto Rotenturmstrasse with its many shops and eateries. The rooftop bar offers a breathtaking view of the old city.

5
LUXURY & ROMANTIC
hotels

426 HOTEL IMPERIAL

Kärntner Ring 16
Innere Stadt ① ④
+43 (0)1 501 100
imperialvienna.com

The hotel was originally built for the Fürst von Württemberg as a private palace and later converted into a hotel along famous Ringstrasse, Vienna's best address, in 1873. Since then it is the most famous five-star luxury hotel in Vienna, just opposite the Musikverein, where you can hear the best classic concerts in town.

427 HOTEL SACHER

Philharmoniker
Strasse 4
Innere Stadt ①
+43 (0)1 514 561 555
sacher.com

The Sacher is in a league of its own. Not only did it lend its name to the world's most famous cake, the *Sachertorte*, it also is a luxury hotel with a long tradition. The French designer Pierre-Yves Rochon renovated with great respect for this fabulous historic building. Ask Chef-Concierge Wolfgang Buchmann and his team for the best city tips.

428 PARK HYATT VIENNA

Am Hof 2
Innere Stadt ⓘ
+43 (0)1 227 401 234
hyatt.com/en-US/
hotel/austria/park-
hyatt-vienna

A bank that was transformed into a modern luxury hotel. The Park Hyatt Vienna is situated right next to the 'golden quarter' where you can find all the luxury labels. Definitely the best place to go on a mad shopping spree. Visit the elegant restaurant and bar, enjoy the spa and indoor pool and mingle with the rich and beautiful.

429 PALAIS HANSEN KEMPINSKI

Schottenring 24
Innere Stadt ⓘ
+43 (0)1 236 10 00
kempinski.com

Originally built as a hotel for the World Exhibition in 1873, the Hansen Kempinski has been a luxury hotel for over 100 years. It is situated along the famous Ringstrasse, just like the Imperial. It offers 152 rooms and suites, two restaurants and bars and a cigar lounge. Smokers welcome.

430 GRAND HOTEL WIEN

Kärntner Ring 9
Innere Stadt ⓘ
+43 (0)1 515 80-0
grandhotelwien.com

This famous hotel opened in 1870 and is also one of Vienna's Ringstrassen-hotels. It is part of the Leading Hotels of the World. For many years, it was a hub for Viennese high society and international guests but now you can also enjoy its beautiful interior and restaurant as a visitor. Fabulous gourmet dining.

5 rooms
WITH A VIEW

431 SOFITEL VIENNA STEPHANSDOM

Praterstrasse 1
Leopoldstadt ②
+43 (0)1 906 160
sofitel.com/Wien

The Sofitel Vienna looms up like a black monolith, forming a gate between Vienna's first and second district. Black and white are the colours the stark design concept the architect Jean Nouvel developed for this hotel. Enjoy the view of the Donaukanal from the white rooms or the rooftop restaurant Le Loft.

432 HILTON VIENNA

Am Stadtpark 1
Landstrasse ③
+43 (0)1 71 700
www3.hilton.com

Choose the Hilton Vienna to enjoy the perfect combination of a four-star business hotel with a beautiful view of Stadtpark, one of the city's green lungs. Walk to all the main attractions and get to the airport in just 15 minutes. Shopping mall and cinemas nearby.

433 INTERCONTINENTAL WIEN

Johannesgasse 28
Landstrasse ③
+43 (0)1 711 220
intercontinental.com/
Vienna

Visit the Interconti Vienna as long as it is still there. This was Austria's biggest hotel when it was opened in 1964 and its bar is still one of the best in town. Currently the city is discussing its demolition and the reconstruction of the hotel and the nearby Eislaufverein.

434 DO&CO HOTEL VIENNA

Stephansplatz 12
Innere Stadt ①
+43 (0)1 241 88
docohotel.com

This place offers simply the best view of Stephansdom. The Do&Co Hotel Vienna is situated in the Haashaus, opposite one of Vienna's most famous landmarks. The famous architect Hans Hollein planned a modern building that would reflect the dome. A building that caused quite a furore when it was completed in 1990.

435 PARKHOTEL SCHÖNBRUNN

Hietzinger Haupt-
strasse 10
Hietzing ⑧
+43 (0)1 878 046 03
austria-trend.at/de/
hotels/parkhotel-
schonbrunn

The Parkhotel Schönbrunn was originally designed as an elegant guesthouse for the Emperor's guests. It is located opposite Schönbrunn Zoo. You overlook the park and can see Schönbrunn castle from there. Enjoy the imperial charm and dance a waltz in the beautiful historic ballroom.

The 5 best places to sleep on a
SMALL BUDGET

436 25HOURS HOTEL

Lerchenfelder
Strasse 1-3
Neubau ⑤
+43 (0)1 521 51 0
25hours-hotels.com

The slogan of this place is 'We are all mad here'. Come as you are. Essentially this is an informal, relaxed place full of young people. The hotel is very open, inviting a young crowd to the rooftop bar, which often has DJs and dancing. Cheap drinks, with rooms starting from 100 euro.

437 WOMBATS CITY HOSTEL

Mariahilfer
Strasse 137
Rudolfsheim-
Fünfhaus ⑪
+43 (0)1 897 23 36
wombats-hostels.com

There are two wombats in Vienna. We prefer The Lounge near Westbahnhof, so you are near public transport and Vienna's largest shopping street, the Mariahilfer Strasse. If you are travelling alone, this is the perfect place to stay. You'll soon get to know somebody here. A good place to socialise.

438 WIEN MYRTHENGASSE

Myrthengasse 7
Neubau ⑤
+43 (0)1 523 631 60
oejhv.at

What was travelling like before Airbnb? The Österreichischer Jugendherbergs-verband is a member of Hostelling International, the biggest nonprofit organisation for cheap accommodation, with 60 hostels in Austria. Myrthengasse is one of them. If you want to fight gentrification, then book at their places.

439 WESTEND CITY HOSTEL

Fügergasse 3
Mariahilf ⑤
+43 (0)1 597 67 29
viennahostel.at

This is the right place for the young and anybody who feels young. There's no difference. They have singles, doubles and family rooms. You can also book as a group. The hostel is located near Mariahilfer Strasse. The staff is very friendly and international: from Poland, Iran, Turkey, Armenia and several other countries.

440 SCHLOSSHERBERGE WIEN

Savoyenstrasse 2
Ottakring ⑯
+43 (0)1 481 03 00
hostel.at

Schlossherberge means Palace Hostel – which seems like a contradiction. But you'll find that they deliver on their promise. The hostel is located on beautiful Wilhelminenberg, overlooking the whole quarter, in a park and is very eco-friendly. Starting at 25 euro a night for a double room, this is also a good option for families.

436 25HOURS HOTEL

5

UNUSUAL PLACES
to sleep

441 MAGDAS HOTEL

Laufbergergasse 12
Leopoldstadt ②
+43 (0)1 720 02 88
magdas-hotel.at

Magdas is different! Situated in the middle of the beautiful Prater gardens this hotel is run by refugees and profis. They speak 23 different languages here. You can feel the open mindset the minute you walk in. 88 rooms with an upcycling design, every one is unique and exceptional. Just like us.

442 HOTEL KUNSTHOF

Mühlfeldgasse 13
Leopoldstadt ②
+43 (0)1 214 31 78
hotelkunsthof.at

The Kunsthof was an art hotel before the term existed. It is a hotel and a gallery too. They combine 115 years of experience with the spirit of modern art. Artists often like to stay here. Have breakfast in the green courtyard.

443 DER WILHELMSHOF

Kleine Stadtgut-
gasse 4
Leopoldstadt ②
+43 (0)1 214 552 10
derwilhelmshof.com

Der Wilhelmshof is an eco-friendly art hotel. Here you will not just find works of art in your room, the rooms are actually art, and were designed by artists like Ty Waltinger and Andreas Reimann. Even the garage was designed by artists. But this house is not a museum, you can use it. Enjoy!

444 HOTEL DANIEL

Landstrasser
Gürtel 5
Landstrasse ③
+43 (0)1 901 310
hoteldaniel.com

Once upon a time the Daniel was an ordinary hotel near the city's central station, but then they rebranded themselves, and since then they are the hottest place in time. A boat by the artist Erwin Wurm graces their roof, telling you everything you need to know about this hotel. Sleep in room 777, a silver retro trailer parked in front of the hotel.

445 GRÄTZLHOTEL KARMELITERMARKT

Every room in
a different place
Leopoldstadt ②
+43 (0)1 208 39 04
graetzlhotel.com

Grätzl means hood. The Grätzlhotel is located in former shops in different places in the city. Their original use is reflected in the modern design. The Urbanauts hospitality group is in charge of this unconventional hotel. Check-in starts at the key safe at Grosse Sperlgasse 6. Then you use your personal code to find your suite.

SEGEL UND SURFSCHULE WIEN

40 PLACES
TO HANG OUT ON
WEEKENDS

5 great places for
CANOEING & SAILING

---

446 SEGEL & SURFSCHULE WIEN

Florian-Berndl-
Gasse 34
Donaustadt ⑦
+43 (0)1 203 67 43
segelschule-wien.at

This family business has been into boats since 1898. At the time, Austria still had a navy. Andreas Irzl's grandfather built various types of boats. Since the sixties, the family has organised sailing courses. As the Uno-City is near, they started to teach in English early on. You can also rent a boat here.

447 BOOTSVERMIETUNG EPPEL

Wagramer
Strasse 48-A
Donaustadt ⑦
+43 (0)1 263 35 30
eppel-boote.at

Eppel is the right place to rent various types of boats. They have electric boats, pedal boats and rowboats. As motorboats are not allowed on the Alte Donau, the atmosphere is totally relaxed. Take your electric boat and have a picnic on the river. You won't get lost because the water is stagnant.

448 SCHINAKL BOOTSVERMIETUNG

Laberlweg 19
Donaustadt ⑦
+43 (0)680 553 49 55
meine-insel.at

There are various options for renting a boat on the Alte Donau, but you can only get to islands at Schinakl Bootsvermietung. They rent a new type of electric boat that is round and has a sofa and a palm tree on it. The perfect place to have a party or celebrate a birthday. The islands are a Viennese design and eco-friendly.

449 ARWEX

Am Rollerdamm 2
Floridsdorf ⑦
+43 (0)1 263 71 11
arwex.at

Here you can improve your paddling technique with experts. Take a two-hour training session or come in the evening from 5 to 7 pm for two days. You can also rent canoes and kayaks. They often organise tours on the Donau and some other nearby rivers like Traisen or Kamp.

450 ARGONAUTEN

An der unteren
Alten Donau 21
Donaustadt ⑦
argowien.at

The Viennese Argonauten rowing club was founded in 1909. There are various rowing clubs around Alte Donau, but some of them are not so open to guests. As the boats are very expensive, you do have to be a club member. The Argonauten are different. They organise a lot of *schnupper* hours.

5

HIKING TOURS

in the city

---

451 KAHLENBERG

Döbling ⑩
wien.gv.at

You can do a lot of hiking without leaving the city, which is quite unique. Use public transport to get to Döbling and climb up Kahlenberg. The mountain (484 meters) is part of the Wienerwald. On top you can find Stephanienwarte, from where you have a splendid view over the city.

452 LEOPOLDSBERG

Döbling ⑩
wien.gv.at

Maybe nearby Leopoldsberg is even more beautiful. You can see the Donau and the vineyards. The mountain was first settled in the 9th century before Christ. People also lived on the mountaintop in the Middle Ages. Leopold I ordered that a church be erected here in 1679. A place with a long history.

453 BISAMBERG

Floridsdorf ⑦
wien.gv.at

From Leopoldsberg you can see Bisamberg on the opposite bank of the Donau. You can start your hike in Stammersdorf/Floridsdorf (go there by tram or bus). The animals and vegetation are completely different from the Wienerwald. No woods, but shrubs and lots of vineyards. It's an environmentally-protected zone.

454 SOPHIENALPE

Penzing
wien.gv.at/
wanderweg8

Sophienalpe is named after Sophie, the mother of Emperor Franz Joseph. She loved to spend time here in summer time when it can get very hot in the city. There are lots of hiking trails here. Children love to toboggan here in winter. Take a 30-minute walk from the car park to the Mostalm where you can eat and drink.

455 WILHELMINENBERG

Ottakring ⑪
wien.gv.at

On the summit of this beautiful mountain you can find a castle, which is now a hotel. In 1781, a first castle was built, but it was rebuilt in 1908 in a neo-empire style. In the sixties, it was a children's home where children were abused, a dark chapter in its history. You wouldn't believe it when you see this beautiful place today.

453 BISAMBERG

5 beautiful
BOAT TRIPS

---

456 NATIONALPARK BOOT

Innere Stadt /
Salztorbrücke ①
+43 (0)1 4000 494 95
donauauen.at

There are not that many cities where you start your boat trip in the city and find yourself in a national park within half an hour. Vienna is one of these. Book a half day trip (4,5 hours) with Nationalpark Boot. When you arrive in Lobau, take a walk in the forest with a ranger. From May to October.

457 TWIN CITY LINER

Innere Stadt /
Motto am Fluss ①
+43 (0)1 904 88 80
twincityliner.com

Vienna and Bratislava in Slovakia are twin cities. Only 80 kilometres separate them. Under the Austrian-Hungarian monarchy a tram connected the cities. Since the fall of the Iron Curtain, you can easily get there by train. But the most beautiful way is by boat, in this case a catamaran.

458 BLUE DANUBE RUNDFAHRT

ddsg-blue-danube.at

Donaudampfsschifffahrtskapitänskajütentür-schnallengriff is perhaps the longest word in German. Ddsg stands for *Donaudampf-schiffahrt* and means steamboat company on the Donau. The rest of the word means the door handle of the captain's cabin. Learn this word by heart during a round trip on the Donau.

459 CITY CRUISE

Schwedenplatz
Innere Stadt ①
+43 (0)1 588 80

You can book this architectural city cruise which focusses on the historic buildings of Otto Wagner or more modern ones – by Zaha Hadid or Jean Nouvel. Enjoy the combination of an interesting architectural tour with a meal in the à-la-carte restaurant on board.

460 BOOTSTAXI

Donaukanal /
Salztorbrücke
Innere Stadt ①
+43 (0)664 201 70 96
bootstaxi.com

If you have money to spend then why not book your own individual boat trip on the Donau. And yes, the MS Skorpion you can book is the Nationalpark Boot. The only difference is that you get to decide where you want to go. 200 euro an hour, for groups of up to 25 people. Choose a full moon trip. It's magical.

5
NATIONAL & BIOSPHERE PARKS *to explore*

461 WIENERWALD
bpww.at

Wienerwald is around 45 kilometres long and 20 up to 30 metres wide. Nowadays almost the entire area is a so-called biosphere park. The Viennese love to spend their weekend having a picnic here or going for a walk. Read Ödön von Horváth's *Tales from the Vienna Woods* about a bitter love story.

462 NEUSIEDLER SEE
nationalpark-neusiedlersee.org

You must leave Vienna to get to Neusiedler See but it is only an hour by train. The lake is called the Viennese seaside as we have no real sea. This lake is a real paradise for many different bird species because of the Pannonian plane (part of the lake is in Hungary). Go bird-watching or take a guided safari.

463 DONAU-AUEN
donauauen.at

This national park to the south of Vienna is one of the last protected wildlife and nature areas of its kind in Europe. It was endangered in 1984 following plans for a hydroelectric power station but protesters prevented this. This marked the beginning of the green movement in Austria.

464 SCHLOSS MARCHEGG
schloss.marchegg.at

The March is a river near Vienna today, and forms the border with Slovakia. Schloss Marchegg is a baroque castle, but there were several castles here before it that were burnt down and destroyed again. Today it is famous for the storks that arrive every year in March.

465 NATURPARK PURKERSDORF
naturparks.at

Naturpark Purkersdorf spans 77 hectares and is very close to the city. Purkersdorf itself is a small town to the south of Vienna, which is famous for its wines. A perfect combination of enjoying nature and wine-tasting. Children will love the petting zoo.

5 of the best
PICNIC SPOTS

---

466 AUGARTEN

Augarten
Leopoldstadt ②

Augarten is a picturesque baroque park in Vienna's second district, Leopoldstadt. It is the home of the famous Wiener Sängerknaben and the Viennese Porcelain Manufactory. So you already have two reasons to visit the park. The third: it's a perfect place for a picnic under large old trees.

466 AUGARTEN

467 NUSSBERG
Eichelhofweg
Döbling ⑲

Nussberg is a small mountain near Nussdorf Village, which is now part of Vienna. It is surrounded by vineyards. It was once covered with walnut trees as the name indicates. Today it is famous for its 'Gemischter Satz', a white wine made of different vines. Not a cuvee. Do taste it.

468 AM HIMMEL
Himmelstrasse 125
Döbling ⑲

Am Himmel means 'in heaven' – and you really feel as if you are. From here you overlook the entire city. Visit the tree circle. When it is crowded, just take a walk along Himmelstrasse where you can find a quiet place to yourself. Easy to get to with bus 39A.

469 PRATER
Arenawiese
Leopoldstadt ②

There are so many different places to meet in Prater. Arenawiese is where the young and alternative crowd hang out. You see'll lots of slackliners showing off their acrobatic stunts. Sometimes there is music or people celebrating their birthday. No fires, no dogs.

470 WILHELMINENBERG
Savoyenstrasse 2
Ottakring ⑰

Ottakring was and still is a working-class district. When you don't walk to the castle at the top of the hill, you can see another side of Wilhelminenberg that is down-to-earth, rustic and quaint. Wander around, go to one of the Heuriger which are frequented by locals or have a picnic.

5 all-level
YOGA STUDIOS

471 YOGAWERKSTATT

Grosse Mohren-
gasse 23/2a
Leopoldstadt ②
+43 (0)699 116 051 47
yogawerkstatt.at

Don't speak, breathe! You will feel the spirit of this place as soon as you enter. Romana and Sascha Delberg created a real refuge in a hidden backyard in Leopoldstadt. They teach Ashtanga and Hatha yoga here. Time for a *schnupper* hour. Every Thursday evening they also host an open meditation.

472 VERONIKA WINKLER STUDIO

Neubaugasse 7
Neubau ⑤
+43 (0)699 101 101 04
veronikawinkler.at

Veronika's studio feels like home. In fact, it is her home. You practise yoga in her open, light apartment. She is a very experienced Iyengar yoga teacher, going into detail when working with you. Enjoy the small classes (maximum 15 participants). You can pay by the hour. All levels.

473 YOGA KULA

Bösendorferstrasse 9
Innere Stadt ① ④
+43 (0)1 504 64 15
yogakula.at

'Where body meets soul' is the slogan of this yoga studio in the city. Just come, no booking required. Check the online timetable though. The studio is open all year long, during the winter and summer holidays, on weekends and public holidays. They have a yoga class here every day.

474 YOGA MELANGE

Thaliastrasse 2/11-12
Ottakring ⑪
+43 (0)699 171 098 83
yogamelange.at

Yoga Melange, like the name tells, is a mix of different yoga styles. Here they teach Ashtanga yoga, Viyasa Krama yoga, Vinyasa Flow yoga as well as the softer Yin yoga where you stay in an Asana for several minutes. Very friendly atmosphere, lots of space, all levels, beginners welcome.

475 INSTITUT DR. SCHMIDA

Lehárgasse 1/2
+43 (0)1 587 50 46
Naschmarkt ④
schmida.com

Schmida has been in business since 1934. It was founded by Susanne Schmida in 1934 as a place for expressive dance and meditation. They have always focussed on the body and soul here, teaching yoga years before it became a hype. They are very spiritual and also teach trance, Sufism, tai chi and much more.

471 YOGAWERKSTATT

5 places to take
DANCING CLASSES

---

476 AIALA GONZALES
AT: AUX GAZELLES
Rahlgasse 5
Mariahilf ⑤
+43 (0)676 408 29 98
wien-im-tanz.com

Aiala Gonzales comes from Basque Country. Since 2012, she has been a fixture on the Viennese tango scene, creating and organising various new milongas. In winter in Aux Gazelles in an ambience inspired by the orient, in summer in open air in front of beautiful Karlskirche. Take a class here.

477 TANGOACADEMIA
AT: TANGOLOFT
Cothmannstrasse 9
Meidling ⑧
tangoacademia.at

Learn to dance the tango with Pablo and Maria in Tangoloft. This place is more than a dance studio. Here you really experience the spirit of tango. It is a friendly space, with plenty of style and flair but don't be deterred. They also welcome beginners. Easy to get to with public transport (U6 Meidling exit Schedifkaplatz).

478 CROSSOVER-MILONGA

Obere Viadukt-
gasse 2
Landstrasse ③
+43 (0)676 476 09 15
crossovermilonga.com

Susanne Maurer is DJ Soozie. Since 2004 she has been organising the open-air crossover milonga with Martin Haslehner in front of Hofburg in Burggarten, a magical place. She is known for her experimental music. Take a class or workshop with her. Women as leader welcome.

479 IG HOP

Vereinsgasse 33/30
Leopoldstadt ②
ighop.at

Lindy Hop is the hot ticket in town. IG Hop was one of the first organisations to organise courses and events in Vienna like the Tuesday Hop in Wirr or the Fruity Hop in Volksgarten Pavillon on Mondays. Sign up for a workshop or just join an event. There often give free lessons before they start.

480 TANZSCHULE ELMAYER

Bräunerstrasse 13
Innere Stadt ①
+43 (0)1 512 71 97
elmayer.at

Noblesse oblige. Elmayer is famous in town and maybe the most traditional dancing school. Here you can take all kinds of courses, for students, seniors, couples and singles. For beginners and pros. In only three hours they can ensure that you're ready for a Viennese ball, the traditional dancing events. Learn all about waltzing and etiquette.

5

DAY SPAS &
WELLNESS TEMPLES

481 AUX GAZELLES HAMMAM

Rahlgasse 5
Mariahilf ⑤
+43 (0)1 585 66 45
auxgazelles.at

You don't have to travel to Istanbul to visit a hammam. Aux Gazelles has a very luxurious one. It is not a traditional one, but women and men have separate areas of course (check the online timetable). When you enter, you receive a *Pestemal* (cotton cloth) and *Kese* (scratch glove). Book a peeling or a massage.

482 THERME WIEN

Kurbadstrasse 14
Favoriten ⑨
+43 (0)1 680 09
thermewien.at

Therme Wien in Oberlaa used to be a bit old-fashioned. But things changed after it reopened. Now it has several in and outdoor pools. They have various saunas, including a nude sauna and a Scandinavian one. Or if you like, a less hot Turkish bath. No children in the sauna area. Easy to get to with U1.

483 THE RITZ CARLTON SPA

Schubertring 5-7
Innere Stadt ①
+43 (0)1 311 88
ritzcarlton.at

If you are in search for a more exclusive day spa, go to the Ritz Carlton. Here they have a whirlpool and you can book your own private Turkish bath (40 euro for three hours). Spa treatments start at 120 euro. The elegant private Spa Suite costs 360 euro for three hours.

484 SANS SOUCI

Burgggasse 2
Neubau ⑤
+43 (0)1 522 25 20
sanssouci-wien.com

A city trip is fun. But it may be stressful sometimes. Step inside to escape the busy streets. Sans Souci is located near MuseumsQuartier making it a great place to unwind for a few hours. A 450-square-metre spa, with a purifying steam bath, several saunas and the warming rays of the sun meadow.

485 DHEVARI SPA

Berggasse 18
Alsergrund ⑥
+43 (0)1 319 88 99
dhevari.at

Dhevari Spa was the first Asian luxury spa in Vienna, so you can book plenty of eastern treatments here including a Shiro-Abhyanga as well as a Royal Thai or a Balinese hot-stone massage. It is open Tuesday to Sunday from 11 am to 10 pm, making it the perfect place to unwind in the evening. Open on public holidays, too.

481 AUX GAZELLES HAMMAM

WIENFLUSS

15 RANDOM FACTS AND URBAN DETAILS

5
STOLPERSTEINE
to look out for

---

486 HAIDGASSE 3

Leopoldstadt ②
+43 (0)681 065 43 14
*steineder
erinnerung.net*

The twelfth station of the *Weg der Erinnerung*, the path of remembrance, in Vienna's second district Leopoldstadt. The Stones of Remembrance Association wishes to keep alive the memory of the many Jewish people who lived here before the Holocaust. You can find these golden plaques in every district.

487 PORZELLAN-GASSE 49-A

Alsergrund ⑥

Part of the project's objective is to ensure their names become visible in public space – to show that something has changed in Vienna and Austria. The association wants to raise the awareness of the people who walk past these stones by making them reflect on history.

488 ANNAGASSE 3-A

Innere Stadt ①

If you are searching for someone specific, you can enter their name in the online database at *steinedererinnerung.net*. If you don't have a name, you can search by district and you will get a list of all the stones of remembrance.

489 BRÜNNER-STRASSE 43
Floridsdorf ⑦

Get to know the story of Gerda and Jenny Feldmann at Brünnerstrasse 43. You will find these plaques in front of the houses where Jewish people lived in or at their last address in Vienna before they were killed or deported. There are also some publications available in English about their plight.

490 HÜTTELDORFER-STRASSE 117
Penzing ⑪

You'll find more plaques in Leopoldstadt as this district was predominantly Jewish. But it is worth exploring other districts too. If you wish a stone or plaque to be installed, you can sponsor the memory of a victim whose relatives are no longer alive for 150 euros or make a donation so the path can be continued.

STOLPERSTEINE

5
LOST RIVERS
in Vienna

---

491 WIENFLUSS

Penzing ⑪
gruengraetzlwege.at

The Wien River was quite large and wild. On old maps (from around 1790) you can see how the river used to wind its way through the city right through Karlsplatz with its famous Karlskirche. In 1898, it was covered over so most of its course is no longer visible although you can still see part of it in Stadtpark.

492 LIESING

Liesing ⑧

The eight villages that form Liesing, Vienna's 23rd district, are situated in the south of the city. Liesing is also the name of the river. It was first referenced in 1002 as Liezniccha, a Slavic word for river in the woods. It is 30 kilometres long but today you can only see parts of it above-ground.

493 **ALSBACH**
Innere Stadt ①

Like so many other rivers the Als is quite a wild river, which begins in the woods around Vienna. It originally flowed through Hernals, Penzing and Währing right to the Donaukanal. When you walk through Tiefer Graben in the city today, bear in mind that it was submerged until 1440.

494 **FAHNENSTANGEN-WASSER**
Leopoldstadt ②

Ask people about Fahnenstangenwasser and most people in Vienna aren't even aware that it ever existed. It originally was a branch of the Donau and flowed to the north of the present-day Augarten, where wood would be brought on land. As the river's water levels tended to fluctuate, they were marked with *Fahnenstangen* (flagpoles).

495 **MARCHFELDKANAL**
Floridsdorf ⑦

As the city lost so many rivers, it created a new one. The Marchfeldkanal is a man-made river. As Marchfeld is a rather dry region to the east of Vienna, but very important for agriculture, this channel was built to irrigate the land. Nowadays it's also a beautiful recreational area.

5 fun facts about
WORLD EXPO
1873

---

496 DOGENHOF

Praterstrasse 70
Leopoldstadt ②
*wiener-
weltausstellung.at*

The gates to the fifth World Expo swung open in Vienna in 1873. It was simply spectacular. Most of the buildings were since demolished, except for a few like Dogenhof. This building reminds us of a time when Vienna resembled Venice and when you could make your way up the Prater in a gondola. Nowadays there is a coffeehouse in Dogenhof.

497 ROTUNDE

The Viennese Rotunde was built in 1873 in Prater. At the time, it had the world's largest domed structure, with a diameter of 108 metres. It was even bigger than the Pantheon in Rome and was considered extraordinary at the time. It burnt down in 1937 but lives on in different songs, the so-called *Wienerlieder*.

498 INDUSTRIEPALAST

The Industriepalast was also built for the *Weltausstellung* in 1873, to the left and right of the central Rotunde, with a total length of 960 metres. It was the main building of the world expo and was destroyed that same year. Nowadays the WU-Campus is located here (see chapter Buildings).

499 PERSISCHES HAUS

There were 194 pavilions at the world expo, with different types of houses showing how people lived under the Austrian-Hungarian monarchy – and around the world. So visitors could see typical Tirolean farms here as well as houses from Croatia, Romania, Russia and Africa. The Persian house was a highlight. We only have pictures of it now.

500 KAISERPAVILLON

When the Expo opened on 1 May 1873, the Kaiserpavillon was far from ready. The building, which had been erected for the Emperor, was decorated with masses of flowers, but even that proved insufficient to conceal the fact that it remained unfinished. Ultimately the Emperor only visited the pavilion in August. If anything it teaches us one thing, namely that architects have a different concept of time.

INDEX

COLOPHON

EDITING *and* COMPOSING — Tanja Paar — www.tanjapaar.at
GRAPHIC DESIGN — Joke Gossé and Sarah Schrauwen
PHOTOGRAPHY — Heribert Corn — www.corn.at
COVER IMAGE — Arena Wien (secret 379)

The addresses in this book have been selected after thorough independent research
by the author, in collaboration with Luster Publishers. The selection is solely based
on personal evaluation of the business by the author. Nothing in this book was
published in exchange for payment or benefits of any kind.

D/2018/12.005/11
ISBN 978 94 6058 2295
NUR 512, 510

© 2018 Luster, Antwerp
www.lusterweb.com — www.the500hiddensecrets.com
info@lusterweb.com

Printed in Italy by Printer Trento.